QUIET TIME

YEAR
DAILY
DEVOTIONAL
grades 5-6

Quiet Time
One year daily devotional for children in grades 5-6

Published by Word of Life Local Church Ministries
A division of Word of Life Fellowship, Inc.
>Joe Jordan - Executive Director
>Don Lough - Director
>Jack Wyrtzen & Harry Bollback - Founders
>Mike Calhoun - VP of Local Church Ministries

USA
P.O. Box 600
Schroon Lake, NY 12870
1-888-932-5827
talk@wol.org

Canada
RR#8/Owen Sound
ON, Canada N4K 5W4
1-800-461-3503 or (519) 376-3516
lcm@wol.ca

Web Address: www.wol.org

Publisher's Acknowledgements
Writers and Contributors: Betsi Calhoun, Beverly Deck, Amy Speck
Editor: Betsi Calhoun
Project Manager: Tim Filler
Cover Design: Sally Robison
Page layout and design: Sally Robison and Beth Shoultz

ISBN - 978-1-931235-60-0
Printed in the United States of America

God Loves You and Wants to Spend Time with You!

Quiet Time is a special time that you set aside each day to read God's Word to get to know Him better and to learn how He wants you to live. During this time, God speaks to you through His Holy Word the Bible and you speak to God through prayer. As a Christian, spending this time everyday is very important for you to grow closer to God.

The Champion Quiet Time will help you have a special time each day with the Lord. This booklet is divided into two sections. A Personal Prayer Diary section where you can write prayer requests to remind yourself to pray for people that you care about and things that are happening. The second section Is the Quiet Time Activity Pages. Activities are written from the Bible verses for each day of the year to challenge you to understand the truths from God's Word.

The Champion Quiet Time and the Teen/Adult Quiet Time use the same Scriptures for the week. This makes it easier for your whole family to discuss the passages together.

This Quiet Time is a great opportunity for you to have fun together with your child. Here are some tips to help your child with their Quiet Time.

>> Gather supplies needed for activities.

>> Sit down at a prescribed time each day.

>> Use the Bible to look up references together.

>> Talk through the activity and personal application.

>> Complete the week by documenting how many days were completed and writing an encouraging note.

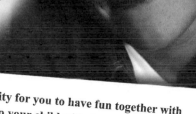

YOUR DAILY QUIET TIME

Begin the week by reading the overview. This will give you a hint about what you will learn that week. Extra facts will increase your understanding of the week's passage.

Each day, read the **Daily Scripture Passage.**

Complete the activity for the day.

Write down your prayer requests in your diary and talk to God in prayer.

Each day concludes with the **Make Your Choice** section for personal application.

WEEK 6

WEEKLY PASSAGES COVERED
EPHESIANS 1:1-2:22

DO YOU KNOW WHERE YOU ARE?

IN EPHESIANS, PAUL WANTS TO ASSURE BELIEVERS THAT THEY ARE "IN CHRIST"—SECURE IN HIM!

HOW MANY TIMES IN CHAPTER 1 CAN YOU FIND THE PHRASES "IN CHRIST", "IN HIM", OR "IN WHOM"? _____

AS A BELIEVER, I LIVE IN CHRIST (1:1-2:6) AND HE LIVES IN ME (2:22)!

Sunday EPHESIANS 1:1-6

TAKE THE CHALLENGE

HAVE YOU EVER WAITED TO SEE IF YOU WILL BE CHOSEN FOR A TEAM, A PART IN A PLAY, OR TO DO A SPECIAL JOB?

CHECK IT OUT

WHO has chosen you? _____

WHEN were you chosen? _____

WHAT have you been chosen for? _____

Make YOUR CHOICE

Knowing that Christ has chosen me to be His child should make me want to _____

42

Things needed for my Quiet Time:

>> Bible   >> Quiet Time Diary
>> Pen   >> A quiet place

My Personal Prayer Diary

SPENDING TIME WITH GOD IN PRAYER

Keeping a Personal Prayer Diary is a great way to remind yourself to pray for specific people and things. It also reminds you to thank God and to tell others when He answers your prayers.

Your prayer time should include praying for friends and family. Especially pray for those who don't know Christ as their Savior.

You should also pray for your Christian friends, your relatives and yourself. Pray that you will grow in your Christian life and become what God wants you to be.

Get to know missionaries who serve the Lord in your area or around the world. Ask them for specific prayer requests. Write these on your prayer pages.

Much of your prayer time should be used thanking and praising God. Tell God that you are thankful for your salvation, parents, home, friends, and answers to prayers.
You should praise God for His beautiful creation, His holiness and His greatness.

Some prayer time should include asking God to meet needs such as clothing, food or maybe a job for your dad. Maybe you could ask God to help you be more obedient. You must be careful not to be selfish and ask for things that you want only for you. As you are obedient to God, He will care for your needs.

DAILY PRAYER REQUESTS

Daily prayer requests are those things that you pray for each day. Maybe someone in your family will be traveling one day and you ask God to protect them as they travel. For each request, write the date that you started praying for it and how God answered your prayer.

NAME

DATE

How God Answered

weekly prayer requests

The Weekly Prayer Request Chart can be used to remind you to pray for specific requests either once a week or more often. Write down the names of friends and family members. Don't forget to include those that need to be saved. Put the names of your church leaders and missionaries that you know so that you can remember to pray for them as well. For each request, write the date that you started praying and how God answered your prayer.

FAMILY & FRIENDS

name	date	how God answered

SUNDAY

Missionaries and Church Leaders

I THANK GOD FOR...

I PRAISE GOD FOR...

FAMILY & FRIENDS

name date how God answered

Missionaries and Church Leaders

I THANK GOD FOR... I PRAISE GOD FOR...

FAMILY & FRIENDS

name   date   how God answered

.... ◯ ....
.... ◯ ....
.... ◯ ....
.... ◯ ....
.... ◯ ....
.... ◯ ....
.... ◯ ....
.... ◯ ....
.... ◯ ....
.... ◯ ....

Missionaries and Church Leaders

.... ◯ ....
.... ◯ ....
.... ◯ ....

I THANK GOD FOR...   I PRAISE GOD FOR...

....
....
....
....

13

FAMILY & FRIENDS

name	date	how God answered
....	◯	....
....	◯	....
....	◯	....
....	◯	....
....	◯	....
....	◯	....
....	◯	....
....	◯	....
....	◯	....
....	◯	....

Missionaries and Church Leaders

....	◯	....
....	◯	....
....	◯	....

I THANK GOD FOR...   I PRAISE GOD FOR...

I THANK GOD FOR...	I PRAISE GOD FOR...
....	....
....	....
....	....
....	....

FAMILY & FRIENDS

name	date	how God answered

Missionaries and Church Leaders

I THANK GOD FOR...	I PRAISE GOD FOR...

FAMILY & FRIENDS

name	date	how God answered
....	◯	....
....	◯	....
....	◯	....
....	◯	....
....	◯	....
....	◯	....
....	◯	....
....	◯	....
....	◯	....
....	◯	....

Missionaries and Church Leaders

....	◯	....
....	◯	....
....	◯	....

I THANK GOD FOR...   I PRAISE GOD FOR...

....

....

....

....

FAMILY & FRIENDS

name   date   how God answered

....

....

....

....

....

....

....

....

....

....

Missionaries and Church Leaders

....

....

....

I THANK GOD FOR...   I PRAISE GOD FOR...

....

....

....

....

17

Psalms 26:1-31:24

EMOTIONS... up... down... left...right... Check your heart.... Suit up for battle...

Download God's power and pray!!

Sunday Psalm 26:1-12

TAKE THE CHALLENGE

Is it time for a heart examination?

CHECK IT OUT

How's your heart? In verse 2, the psalmist asks God to examine his heart. What are some things he make a checklist about doing or not doing in verses 3-8?

☐ _____   ☐ _____

☐ _____   ☐ _____   ☐ _____

Now go back through the list you have made.

MAKE YOUR CHOICE

Now, I will check the ones I need to really work on!
I want to change my heart attitudes about:

_____.

monday
Psalm 27:1-14

TAKE THE CHALLENGE Do you ever feel like you are in a battle?

CHECK IT OUT Sometimes it may seem like home, school, time with friends, and even church is a battle ground rather than a safe place. Take heart! The psalmist felt this way, too. Write below how the psalmist felt in verses 2-3 and 11-14: _____

_____

From what was he gaining his confidence? _____

_____

MAKE YOUR CHOICE If I know Jesus as my Savior, I can have confidence in Him! This makes me feel: _____

_____.

Tuesday
Psalm 28:1-9

TAKE THE CHALLENGE What does it mean to be two-faced?

CHECK IT OUT Verse 3 describes what it means to be two-faced. It means that you are kind to someone when you are with them, but you think unkind things about them in your heart and often tell this to others. Fill in the cartoon blocks below with your own cartoon showing how someone can be two-faced.

MAKE YOUR CHOICE Have I ever been two-faced? **Y / N** How? _____

_____ How can I be kind even when I don't feel like it? _____

wednesday — Psalm 29:1-11

Download God's Power!

CHECK IT OUT

Have you ever seen an MP3 player? It's cool how so many songs can fit into such a small space! God is so powerful and has so many facets to His character that even a million songs sung about Him would only scratch the surface of His greatness. Pretend that you are writing song titles about God from today's verses. What would they be called?

glory and strength

MAKE YOUR CHOICE

If I could sing a song to God about how much I love Him I would say_____

_____

Thursday — Psalm 30:1-12

TAKE THE CHALLENGE

Can I get a little help here?

CHECK IT OUT

In today's verses the psalmist is describing God as his help in time of trouble. Search for words from today's verses in the word search below that describe how God helped him.

```
T E V A G R O F I N G L
H G H E A L E D D P A I
G T E A R A O L Y E B F
U J L F U K W O L R P T
O T P I P O B V D K A E
R Y E I K L M A Q N H D
B S D A C O B V D W A D
D E N E H T G N E R T S
```

MAKE YOUR CHOICE

I will rely on Jesus to help me today with this problem:

_____

20

FRIDAY Psalm 31:1-13

Trapped! Cramped! Can't Breathe!

CHECK IT OUT

Have you ever been in a tight place and wondered if you would be able to get out? How about a crowded elevator? Have you ever felt like things going on around you were crowding in on you? God has a promise for you in verse 8. He will set your feet _____ _____. God will _____ you if you will only turn to Him.

MAKE YOUR CHOICE

I am feeling crowded in by_____

_____. I will ask God to help me right now.

SATURDAY Psalm 31:14-24

TAKE THE CHALLENGE

"What time is it, Mr. Wolf?"

CHECK IT OUT

Have you ever played the game that asks, "What time is it, Mr. Wolf?" Time is interesting. Sometimes it flies by, and other times it seems to crawl. Can you think of some of these times? What does the psalmist say about our times in verse 15a? "_____

_____ "

MAKE YOUR CHOICE

How can I use my time for Him today? _____

_____

_____ 21

"Gloom, despair and agony on me!" Trouble is there, but God is close to help! Ever had one of those "terrible, horrible, no good, very bad days"? Well read on! So did David, the songwriter.

Sunday   Psalm 32:1-11

TAKE THE CHALLENGE   What does the guilt of sin feel like?

CHECK IT OUT

David describes what the guilt of his sin felt like to him in verse 4. He said that it felt like God's hand was "_____."

Have you ever felt like this? _____

What did David choose to **do** and **not** do in verse 5? DO: _____

NOT DO: _____

MAKE YOUR CHOICE

When I sin, I need to _____.

What sin do I need to confess to God right now? _____

_____

monday   Psalm 33:1-9

What's the point?

CLUES:
1. You do this to an instrument. (v. 3)
2. This is always right/upright (v. 4)
3. The planet we live on is called (v. 8)
4. The opposite of wrong
5. The opposite of false
6. Look up: you'll see them (v. 6)

The theme for today from the circled letters is ___ ___ ___ ___ ___ ___ ___.

I want to show God that I love and appreciate Him today by:

_____

_____

Tuesday   Psalm 33:10-22

TAKE THE CHALLENGE

Who is watching you?

CHECK IT OUT

Have you seen the computer satellite pictures of earth from space? Or have you looked for your house from out of an airplane window on take-off or landing? It's pretty neat isn't it? Verses 13-15 talk about Who is watching over you from above, and is interested in your life. Write verse 18 here: "_____

_____

_____ "

MAKE YOUR CHOICE

To know that God is watching over me and considering everything I do makes me feel: (circle) happy... safe... scared... guilty... loved... creepy Why? _____

TAKE THE CHALLENGE Do you like Aslan the Lion from the Chronicles of Narnia?

CHECK IT OUT Lions are amazing, aren't they? They are so beautiful, but also extremely powerful and majestic. Verse 10 actually talks about lions, and also holds a promise for you if you know Jesus as your Savior. What does part a of this verse say about lions?

_____

What is the promise (part b) for those who seek the Lord? _____

MAKE YOUR CHOICE When I get older I would like to be a: _____
_____ I will pray now and entrust my dreams and future to God, Who is working for my good. _____

Thursday Psalm 34:11-22

TAKE THE CHALLENGE I'm a Christian, so it's smooth sailing for me!

CHECK IT OUT What does verse 19 tell you about the life of a righteous person? They will have many _____.

What is God's promise to that person? "_____
_____ "

What is God's promise to the person who is brokenhearted in verse 18? "_____ "

MAKE YOUR CHOICE God, sometimes my life seems easy, and sometimes it is really hard and it hurts. Today my life is (a) smooth, things are going well (b) hard, things are rough. Today I want to pray about_____,
and I want to praise You for _____.

FRIDAY

Psalm 35:1-14

Stick up for me!

In today's passage, David is really being picked on by others. How do you know this? Pick out some word clues that describe his situation: _____

_____

Now pick out some words that describe how he would like God to help him: _____

_____

Have I ever been picked on for being a Christian and standing up for Jesus? What happened... _____.

What are some other ways I could be a witness for Jesus? _____

_____

SATURDAY

Psalm 35:15-28

Fight for me!

Again, David is asking God to fight for him and defend him against his enemies who continue to make his life miserable. David asks the Lord to come to his aid. Find the words in the word search below that tell how David would like God to help him.

```
L R U B L E S S I N G
V I N D I C A T E P C
A S S A R A L I Y E O
E E D F U K O R L E N
K A E P S O B V D K T
A Y F R E S C U E N E
W E J U D G E V D R N
A R E T H D N E F E D
```

awake, rise, vindicate, contend, speak, stir, judge, rescue, defend

Sometimes missionaries and pastors feel like no one is standing with them. Who is a missionary that I could pray for right now? _____

I will also pray for Pastor _____. 25

3 Psalm 36:1–39:13

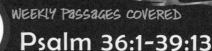

Samuel calls David the "Sweet Psalmist of Israel" or in other Bible versions, "Israel's Singer of Songs" (2 Samuel 23:1). God said he was "a man after mine own heart" (Acts 13:22).

Don't you think it's wonderful that God had David record his thoughts, feelings, and prayers so we can read them? Let's Explore!

Sunday Psalm 36:1-12

TAKE THE CHALLENGE

Do you ever wonder what makes wicked people wicked?

CHECK IT OUT

Fill in the verse number where you find each of these descriptions of the wicked.

He doesn't fear or respect God. ▢

He thinks too much of himself. ▢

He lies and deceives. ▢

He plans to do wrong. ▢

Yet even when people are wicked, God is _____!

I sometimes struggle with the wicked characteristic in verse ▢ . God forgive me and change me!

Psalm 37:1-13

TAKE THE CHALLENGE

Do you fret when you see people getting away with doing wrong?

CHECK IT OUT

David did, too! So what was his "fret not" formula? Write down at least six action verbs from verses 3-8 that helped David deal with it.

_____ _____ _____

_____ _____ _____

MAKE YOUR CHOICE

The next time I am frustrated by someone getting away with something, I will _____

_____, just like David said!

Tuesday   Psalm 37:14-26

TAKE THE CHALLENGE

Are you ever tempted to be stingy or selfish?

CHECK IT OUT

Circle the correct answer for each of the following

Verse 21: Do the wicked   **take or give?**

Verses 21 & 26: Do the righteous   **take or give?**

Verses 25, 26 & 28: Does God   **take or give?**

MAKE YOUR CHOICE

Today, I can open my heart and share (What?) _____

_____ with (Who?) _____,

because I know God generously meets my needs!

27

TAKE THE CHALLENGE

CHECK IT OUT

Who's going to win – the good guys or the bad guys?

ACROSS
4. Who will inherit the land?
6. What does the righteous speak?

DOWN
1. Transgressors or sinners will be _____. (v. 38)
2. Who will be cut off?
3. What the Lord does for the righteous (v. 40)
5. What we are to stay away from?

MAKE YOUR CHOICE

Circle the correct words.
I should be: **NERVOUS** Confident **AFRAID** *Thankful*, knowing that God will win over evil.

TAKE THE CHALLENGE

When you know you have done something wrong, how do you feel?

CHECK IT OUT

In which verses do you find these words that describe how David felt because of his sin? (Put the verse number in each box.)

Like an arrow was stabbing him

Weighed down by a heavy burden

Weak, without strength

Rejected by friends

MAKE YOUR CHOICE

Lord, when I sin I feel_____

A sin I need to confess to You now is _____

FRIDAY — Psalm 38:12-22

TAKE THE CHALLENGE

Do you feel that you have no one to go to when you are overwhelmed by the guilt of something you have done?

CHECK IT OUT

Verses 13-14 say David is like one who can't _____ or _____ because of his sin. Verse 17 says he is about to _____. But who does he hope/wait for (v. 15)? _____

MAKE YOUR CHOICE

Write out verses 18 and 22 as a prayer of confession for your sin

"I _____

_____

_____

_____

_____ "

SATURDAY — Psalm 39:1-13

TAKE THE CHALLENGE

Still feeling bad, sad, confused? What should you do?

CHECK IT OUT

What words from this Psalm express these instructions?

1. BE careful: "_____"

2. BE quiet: "_____"

3. ASk GOd: "_____"

MAKE YOUR CHOICE

God, I may not always understand everything that happens, but I can take comfort in verse 7: "My hope is in _____."

29

4 Psalms 40:1–45:17

Did you know that even though fifty-one of the Psalms have anonymous authors, there are seven authors whom we can trace certain "psalms" or "worship songs" back to? See if you can match each author (draw lines between them) with the number of psalms he wrote (then check the key the last day of this week to see how many you got right).

DAVID   ASAPH   HEMAN   SOLOMON

12   9   1   73   2

SONS OF KORAH   MOSES   ETHAN

Sunday   Psalm 40:1-8

TAKE THE CHALLENGE

Has someone ever promised to do something with you later – but you had to wait for them to keep their promise? How good are you at waiting?

CHECK IT OUT

What did the psalmist David do "for the LORD" here?
w _____ p _____ What did the Lord do in return for David's patience in waiting?

1. "He _____ (un)to me" (v. 1).
2. "He _____ my _____" (v. 1).
3. He lifted me up out of what (v. 2)? _____
4. "He _____ my _____ upon a _____" and made me secure (v. 2b).
5. "He put a _____ _____ in my _____," praise to God (v. 3)!

MAKE YOUR CHOICE

What have I been praying for that God has not answered yet? _____
_____ What might God want to do for me or in me as I wait patiently for HIS will and HIS answers to my prayers?

monday

Psalm 41:1-13

TAKE THE CHALLENGE

Have you ever secretly felt happy when someone else got in trouble?

CHECK IT OUT

David describes his tearful feelings about several types of people in his life in this prayer:
- In verse 1 he talks about the _____ people. What will God do for these hurting people, according to verses 2-3? _____
- In verses 5- 8, David describes his _____. He said they all "_____" against him. Not a fun experience!
- In verse 9, he refers to his own "_____," whom he had _____. But Whom did he care most of all about pleasing? The _____ (See vv. 10-12.)

MAKE YOUR CHOICE

Who do I turn to when my good friend turns against me or hurts me with his words? _____ How does the Lord want me to treat others, no matter who they are? _____ _____

Tuesday

Psalm 42:1-11

TAKE THE CHALLENGE

Have you ever felt really down, depressed, or deeply sad? – What did you do?

CHECK IT OUT

Read all the way through this psalm by the sons of Korah and put a check in your Bible beside each reference these brothers make to being very sad ("tears," "cast down," "in despair," "downcast," "mourning," "disquieted," "disturbed,"). How many times did they mention their sadness, hurt, or pain in these verses? _____ But even in their sadness, Whom did their soul "thirst" for? "the _____ _____" They also trusted that God would command (direct) His _____ in the _____ and His _____ in the nighttime. They ended by telling us to put our "_____ in GOD!"

MAKE YOUR CHOICE

What has been one of the saddest times for me in the past year? _____ What can I do about it the next time I go through a painful, sad time in my life?

_____

31

wednesday — Psalm 43:1-5

TAKE THE CHALLENGE

How would you finish this sentence: "God is MY _____."

CHECK IT OUT

First, look back at the psalm you read yesterday and write down the verse numbers from today's psalm and yesterday's that are exactly the same! Psalm 42: _____ and Psalm 43: _____ At least three times in this short psalm, the writer calls God "MY" something. Read through it and write down each time he does this. God is "MY" _____, _____ and _____.

MAKE YOUR CHOICE

If I had to tell someone else who doesn't know God personally, what He means to me, what would I want to tell them first? _____

Thursday — Psalm 44:1-14

TAKE THE CHALLENGE

Has there been a time in your Christian life where God seemed really far away? Like He wasn't listening to you anymore? Like He didn't care?

CHECK IT OUT

This psalm is in four parts. We are looking at the first two parts today. In verses 1-8 the sons of Korah are recounting the good things God had done for Israel in the past. Write down one of those good things they describe: "_____." Now, look at their change of tone in verses 9-14. They start off verse 9 by telling God off: "But (yet) _____."

MAKE YOUR CHOICE

What might I say to God in those times where I feel He has forgotten me or allowed something painful in my life? _____ Does God listen and care even when I am angry at Him and don't understand? **Yes / No**

FRIDAY — Psalm 44:15-26

TAKE THE CHALLENGE

Did you know it's okay to tell God exactly how you feel, even when it's not very positive or worshipful? Many great saints of the Bible have questioned God in their pain and cried out to him. Even JESUS, on the cross, said, "My God, my God, ,WHY hast Thou forsaken me?"

CHECK IT OUT

In the chart below, put the negative (complaining) comments the sons of Korah make to God on one side and the positive (happy) ones on the other side.

_____   _____
_____   _____
_____   _____
_____   _____

MAKE YOUR CHOICE

It was obvious from doing the chart above that these brothers were looking for the negative more than the positive. How can I focus more on the positive in my life today? _____

SATURDAY — Psalm 45:1-17

TAKE THE CHALLENGE

When's the last time you went to a wedding? What did you enjoy the most about it?

CHECK IT OUT

This psalm is actually a wedding song by the Korah brothers, written to the tune of a piece called, "Lilies." Near the center of this psalm, the Korah brothers describe the power of God (v. 6):

"_____ _____, O God, is _____ _____ and _____."

In verse 7, we are told that God loves what? _____
_____

What does he hate? _____

MAKE YOUR CHOICE

Write down the great promise the wedding couple made on their big day: "I will _____
_____ generations." (v. 17) The person I marry someday needs to love _____ most of all!

33

Psalm 46:1-50:23

God is.....

GREAT
GUIDE
HELP
JUDGE
KING
MIGHTY
REDEEMER
REFUGE
STRENGTH

```
T L O G R E A T J R
Z A N G K T P Q E M
P I E R N G L M H I
K B J R N N E K I G
R E F U G E H T B H
X U A U D R S Y F T
L R I E L T J Z E Y
X D R N G S L G I O
E N G E G D U J B L
Y Z B E Y P K R T I
```

Sunday Psalm 46:1-11

TAKE THE CHALLENGE

Think of a place where you feel safe.....

CHECK IT OUT

The word "refuge" means "safe place." Substitute this definition in place of the word refuge in verse 1: "God is our _____ _____ and strength." According to verse 7, where is God? "_____ _____"

MAKE YOUR CHOICE

I never need to be _____!

Since God is always with me, I am always in my safe place!

monday

Psalm 47:1-9

TAKE THE CHALLENGE

How would you describe worship?

CHECK IT OUT

Fill in the blanks from verse 1 to see one way God describes worship ___ ___ ___ ___ your hands ___ ___ ___ ___ ___ to ___ ___ ___ Fill in the circles below with the circled letters above. Worship is not always quiet, sometimes it's ___ ___ ___ ___!

MAKE YOUR CHOICE

I'm _____ about what God has done for me, and I want to show it!

Tuesday

Psalm 48:1-14

TAKE THE CHALLENGE

Have you heard the word Zion in songs and wondered what it means?

CHECK IT OUT

Verse 2b tells us what Mount Zion is: "The _____ of the whole _____." Zion is always a word picture for the homeland of God's people. It's also a real city-Jerusalem. What kind of a place is Zion? (Circle the right choices)

Dark?   Or   Happy?
Temporary?   Or   Permanent?
Beautiful?   Or   Ugly?

MAKE YOUR CHOICE

The best part about Zion is that _____ is there. Now I know why we sing about it!

wednesday Psalm 49:1-11

TAKE THE CHALLENGE What can money get for you?

CHECK IT OUT Based on today's passage, fill in the blanks with the words below: We shouldn't be _____, even though we live among _____ people who trust in their _____, who think they can give enough money to _____ to save someone's life, and who think they will live _____.

SAVE/REDEEM   FOREVER   EVIL   AFRAID   MONEY

MAKE YOUR CHOICE What kind of people in my life should I spend time with?
_____

Thursday Psalm 49:12-20

TAKE THE CHALLENGE Have you ever heard the saying "You can't take it with you"?

CHECK IT OUT Which verse in this passage tells us we can't take anything with us when we die?

Since this is true, should we waste our time and energy collecting things and money? _____

MAKE YOUR CHOICE Lord, help me to be _____ for the things you bless me with, and not always wanting more.

FRIDAY — Psalm 50:1-13

TAKE THE CHALLENGE

Who is qualified to be a judge, anyway?

CHECK IT OUT

<u>God</u> is the ultimate judge!

Some of His qualifications are:

He controls the rising and setting of the _____.

The heavens proclaim His _____. He owns

the _____ (v.10), the _____

(v. 11), and the whole _____ (v. 12).

MAKE YOUR CHOICE

If God owns everything, what can I ask Him for?

_____

SATURDAY — Psalm 50:14-23

TAKE THE CHALLENGE

How have you fallen short of God's standards?

CHECK IT OUT

Do you ever:

☐ Hate instruction (v. 17)? (I'm not teachable.)

☐ "Cast my words behind you" (neglect or ignore God's Word) (v. 17)? (Don't do my Quiet Time faithfully.)

☐ Steal or cheat (v. 18)?

☐ Use your mouth for evil (v. 19-20)? (Gossip, talk back to parents, lie.)

Mark the areas that you struggle with.

MAKE YOUR CHOICE

I will write out verse 15 to remind me what God says to do when I struggle with sin: "_____

_____

_____." 37

2 Corinthians 1:1-4:18

The Apostle Paul was a great missionary traveler, but he was also a great letter-writer.

Did you know he wrote a total of thirteen letters that became part of God's Word, the Bible? Nine of those letters were written to churches and four to individuals who were in ministry. Look at the names below and put a square around the individuals he wrote to and a circle around the churches he wrote to.

Romans	Philemon	Ephesians	Timothy
Philippians	Galatians	Colossians	Corinthians
	Thessalonians	Titus	

Sunday   2 Corinthians 1:1-11

TAKE THE CHALLENGE

Think how many thousands of believers have read Paul's letters to churches and individuals over the years. Do you like to write letters? Have you ever written someone to encourage them in their faith?

CHECK IT OUT

Fill in the blanks from today's passage. Who helped Paul write this letter? _____ This letter was written to the _____ of God in _____ _____ together with all the _____ who lived in ____ _____. What two blessings did Paul bestow on the Corinthian believers from God the Father in verse 3b? The Father of _____ and God of _____

MAKE YOUR CHOICE

In verse 11, Paul tells the believers that they were helping him by their prayers. What Christian worker or missionary can I help today by praying for them? _____

38

2 Corinthians 1:12-24

TAKE THE CHALLENGE

What did God give you at salvation that guarantees you are His child?

CHECK IT OUT

Verse 20 reminds us that all God's promises to us in His Word are (circle one) **Yes / No / Maybe** and **Amen / Oh Me / Forget It** in Jesus Christ. I can know I'm God's own child (vs. 21-22) because He _____ us and put His own _____ in our hearts.

MAKE YOUR CHOICE

What does God's Holy Spirit do in my life that reminds me I'm God's child? _____
_____

Tuesday 2 Corinthians 2:1-13

TAKE THE CHALLENGE

When was the last time you said, "I forgive you" to someone who had hurt or misjudged you? Did you really mean it?

CHECK IT OUT

Paul had written his first letter to the church at Corinth (1 Corinthians), instructing them to deal with a certain man in the church who was involved in the sin of immorality and adultery. They had expelled him from their fellowship. But now that he had repented, Paul wanted the Corinthian believers to _____ and to _____ him (v. 7). They were also urged to confirm or reaffirm their _____ for this sorrowful man. According to verse 11, who is always trying to catch us off guard with his tricks? _____

MAKE YOUR CHOICE

What tricks might Satan have "up his sleeve" for me? _____
_____

How will I overcome him? _____

39

wednesday — 2 Corinthians 2:14-3:5

TAKE THE CHALLENGE

Have you ever been in a room with someone wearing strong perfume or cologne?

CHECK IT OUT

Paul uses several dynamic word pictures here to represent victorious Christian living. Circle them below and draw a picture of one of them in the frame.

SWEET, FRAGRANT PERFUME OF CHRIST WHOSE AROMA SPREADS TO ALL --- A FIRE THAT BLAZES--- A SHIP ON THE RAGING SEA --- A TRIUMPHANT VICTORY PROCESSION --- A LETTER FROM CHRIST

MAKE YOUR CHOICE

As God's letter, I am the only Bible some people may ever read. What do other people see about Jesus when they read my life? _____

Thursday — 2 Corinthians 3:6-18

TAKE THE CHALLENGE

How would you define freedom? We all long for it, but many don't understand what it truly is.

CHECK IT OUT

Cross out the things below that do not bring true freedom, and circle those that do represent true freedom or liberty. **MOSES' LEADERSHIP**
TEMPORARY GLORY   THE TEN COMMANDMENTS or LAW
THE SPIRIT OF THE LORD   As we give God's Spirit more and more control of our lives, and get to know Jesus better and better, we are _____ into Jesus' _____. (v. 18) We become more and more like Him each day until we get to Heaven.

MAKE YOUR CHOICE

How is God's Spirit changing my life from day to day?

_____

Do I spend time with Jesus each day? **Yes / No**

FRIDAY — 2 Corinthians 4:1-7

TAKE THE CHALLENGE

Did you ever have an old jar or box in which you kept your special treasures, coins, or saved money in?

CHECK IT OUT

Write out verse 7 below, then write what our treasure inside is, according to these verses.

_____

_____

_____

_____

MAKE YOUR CHOICE

When what's inside of me comes out (my words, actions, expressions), what do others see and know is important to me? _____

SATURDAY — 2 Corinthians 4:8-18

TAKE THE CHALLENGE

Have you ever felt really bad and that you have nowhere to turn for help?

CHECK IT OUT

Complete the crossword from these exciting verses.

1 across: _____ but not in despair (despairing). 2 across: Persecuted (pursued) but _____ forsaken (abandoned). 1 down: Struck or cast down but not _____. 4 across: So that the life of _____ may be revealed or manifest in our (2 down) _____. 3 down: We believe with the same _____ of faith (v. 13). 5 across: Grace will cause thanksgiving to overflow to the _____ of God. 3 across: Inwardly we are _____ day by day.

MAKE YOUR CHOICE

I've been feeling (circle one) perplexed / frustrated / happy / sad / persecuted / forsaken / alone lately. **Who should I turn to with my hurt and pain?** _____

How? _____

41

chrtyrcrs

Do you know what happened between Paul's first and second letters to the Corinthians?

Well, a group of religious troublemakers, headed by a man who opposed Paul, had come over from Jerusalem and tried to tell Christians they had to obey all the Jewish laws and rituals. They called themselves the "Christ party". The very church Paul, himself, had planted there in Corinth had become so infiltrated by false Christianity that Paul was not even welcome there!

Sunday 2 Corinthians 5:1-10

TAKE THE CHALLENGE

Did you ever think about the truth that your earthly body is just a tent or temple for your soul? Someday you'll simply discard it!

CHECK IT OUT

When our "earthly _____" (our human body) is destroyed through death, we have a _____ of (from) _____, an eternal house in _____ awaiting us. The deposit (earnest or guarantee) of our heavenly home is the Holy _____ ___ (v. 5). One of the shortest verses in the Bible is also a wonderful truth. Write out verse 7 on the eyeglasses below " _____ _____ "

MAKE YOUR CHOICE

I can be confident in the future because my real home is _____. I'm actually an alien on planet _____.

2 Corinthians 5:11-21

TAKE THE CHALLENGE

When was the last time you actually told someone about Jesus and how to go to Heaven?

CHECK IT OUT

Can you identify three reasons (from these verses) why we should witness to others about Christ?

1. Verse 11 — Because we know the _____ of the LORD.

2. Verse 14 — The _____ of Christ compels or constrains us. He loved us so much, He _____ for us.

3. Verse 17 — Because we are new _____s in Christ, and all the _____ things and ways have become _____.

MAKE YOUR CHOICE

What's the biggest reason I'm afraid to witness to others about Jesus? _____

What reason for witnessing (see above) will I use to help me witness more faithfully? _____

Leadership

Tuesday   2 Corinthians 6:1-10

TAKE THE CHALLENGE

Sometimes a great leader is one who has endured many hardships. Do you want to be a leader for God?

CHECK IT OUT

Paul went through many hard trials to become a godly leader. Identify at least seven hardships Paul faced and write each on the rungs of the ladder

Servitude

MAKE YOUR CHOICE

Ask your pastor, club coach, or other godly leader what hardships they have gone through that made them better leaders. Write here some key things they shared:

_____

wednesday — 2 Corinthians 6:11–7:1

TAKE THE CHALLENGE Do you know any Christian guys or gals who are good friends with or date unbelievers?

CHECK IT OUT Paul tells the Corinthian believers to "be ye not unequally yoked together with unbelievers" — not to make unbelievers their best friends or their mates. By drawing a line between them, match the opposites with each other (circles with squares) below that show we have nothing in common with unbelievers.

RIGHTEOUSNESS	LIGHT	BELIEVER (HE THAT BELIEVETH)
unbeliever or infidel	wickedness,	Belial (Satan)
CHRIST	unrighteousness	idols
darkness	lawlessness	TEMPLE OF GOD

MAKE YOUR CHOICE Look at 7:1. Instead of having ungodly friendships, I need to _____ myself from everything that could contaminate or defile my life. What is one way I need to do this?_____

_____

Thursday — 2 Corinthians 7:2–16

TAKE THE CHALLENGE Do you have a friend who makes you feel better whenever you're around them?

CHECK IT OUT As you read through these verses, what name (Paul's special friend) pops up two times? _____
In which verses? _____ and _____ This friend of Paul's actually went all the way to Corinth to visit their church and check up on the believers there. What did Titus find out about them? _____ Paul was encouraged or comforted by _____, and Titus was encouraged or "refreshed" by the _____. Paul said he had _____ in the Corinthian believers in every area (v. 16).

MAKE YOUR CHOICE I choose to hang around with what kind of friends? _____ How can I encourage another friend of mine to be more godly? _____

_____

FRIDAY

2 Corinthians 8:1-15

TAKE THE CHALLENGE

How much do you give to God each week, and how do you give it?

CHECK IT OUT

Paul said the Macedonian churches had given much to help other Christians who were in need. They gave out of their own deep (extreme) _____ (v. 2). They were following the example of their Savior, _____, Who had become poor for our sakes so that we "through his _____ might be _____ " (v. 9). Name the five areas in which Paul said the Corinthian Christians excelled or abounded (v. 7): In _____ , in _____, in _____, in _____ and in _____

MAKE YOUR CHOICE

What decision do I need to make about truly giving or sacrificing to God? _____ _____

SATURDAY

2 Corinthians 8:16-24

TAKE THE CHALLENGE

Is there a friend, relative, or church leader in your life who helps challenge you in your Christian walk?

CHECK IT OUT

Paul mentions his special friend, Titus, three times in these verses. Let's make an acrostic with what Paul has told us about him:

T _____ful (7:14 & 8:16)

I nterested in himself / others (circle one) (7:6 & 8:16)

T _____ed with (or accompanied) Paul and Barnabas to many churches (8:19)

U nselfish care/ unfriendly (circle one) (8:16)

S _____ out by Paul to visit the church in Corinth (8:18)

MAKE YOUR CHOICE

What are two ways I could be a better, more encouraging friend? _____ _____

45

WEEKLY PASSAGES COVERED
2 Corinthians 9:1-13:14

What would we see of the old city of Corinth if we flew there for a visit today? We would see a city of ruins, some tall temple columns, the city marketplace, and the actual pavement that formed the floor of the Roman judgment hall. The temple remains would remind us of Corinth's reputation as the center of unspeakable, immoral worship of their goddess of love, Aphrodite.

Sunday 2 Corinthians 9:1-15

TAKE THE CHALLENGE

On a scale of 1-10 (10 being super great) how do you rate your giving to God's work? _____

CHECK IT OUT

(1) This whole chapter is about (circle one):

repenting / giving / preaching

(2) Circle the things that giving to the cause of Christ will do, according to these verses.

Stir others to action / Produce a harvest in your life / Make you a millionaire / Thanksgiving to God / Glorify God / Supplies the needs of God's people / God will more than meet your needs / Show generosity to others

(3) Write out the eight wonderful words of verse 15 on the banner.

MAKE YOUR CHOICE

How can I increase my giving to God's work? _____

_____

46

2 Corinthians 10:1-18

TAKE THE CHALLENGE

Do you know any soldiers who have fought in a real war or battle? Did you know that, as a Christian, you are in a war everyday?

CHECK IT OUT

Even though we live/walk in the _____, we do not _____ like the world or in the flesh. Our weapons that we wage war with are not what (v. 4)? _____ What are they (or should they be)? _____

_____ Every one or our

_____ should be taken captive to the obedience of _____

. Verses 12-18 remind us as warring believers that we shouldn't compare ourselves with _____ or be proud. Instead, verse 17 tells us, "Let him who boasts (glories), boast (or glory) in the _____."

MAKE YOUR CHOICE

How am I preparing myself daily for fighting spiritual battles? _____

_____

Tuesday   2 Corinthians 11:1-15

TAKE THE CHALLENGE

Would you be able to recognize a false teacher or fake Christian if you saw or heard one?

CHECK IT OUT

What was Paul afraid of for these young believers? Look at verse 3. He was afraid that just as _____ was deceived by the trickery of the _____, that their _____ would be led astray or corrupted from the sincere or simple gospel of _____ Then he went on to identify false teachers by two things: they preach a different J_____ than the true one, and they preach a different or false g_____(v. 4). In verse 13, Paul calls these preachers, who pretend to be _____ of Christ, f_____ a_____ and d_____ w_____

MAKE YOUR CHOICE

Verse 14 tells me even Satan disguises himself to look like an angel of light. What has Satan tempted me with that seemed good or fun, but was really wrong? _____

Wednesday — 2 Corinthians 11:16-33

TAKE THE CHALLENGE
Do you know any missionaries who have suffered real persecution for their faith?

CHECK IT OUT
Let's look at who the Apostle Paul was and what he had gone through as he lived out his strong faith in Christ.

WHO AM I (Paul)? (vv. 22-23) + H_ _ _ _ _ + I_ _ _ _ _ _ _ _
+ Descendant of A_ _ _ _ _ _ + Servant/minister of C_ _ _ _ _

5 PERILS OR DANGERS I (Paul) ENDURED: (v.26) (1) _____
(2) _____ (3) _____
(4) _____ (5) _____

WHAT DID I (Paul) SUFFER? (vv. 24-25) ___ times
I received 40 _____ minus one + three
times beaten with _____ + I was _____
+ three times I was _____ + Spent a
night and a day in the _____

What's the worst thing I've ever faced as a Christian?
_____
What missionary who serves in a dangerous place can I pray for right now? _____

Thursday — 2 Corinthians 12:1-10

TAKE THE CHALLENGE
What are the biggest questions you have about Heaven and what it's like?

CHECK IT OUT
In verses 1-6, Paul tells us about his experience fourteen years before of being caught up into the _____ _____. He also described it as being caught up into _____
But Paul also had to deal with a physical handicap or illness ["messenger of Satan"] he called a "_____ in the (my) _____" (v. 7). How many times did he pray God would take this away? (circle one) **5   7   3**

Write out the words of verse 9 below, and then thank God for His sufficient grace in your life. "_____
_____"

FRiDAY · 2 Corinthians 12:11-21

TAKE THE CHALLENGE Have you ever had to try to prove your-self to someone who didn't trust you?

CHECK IT OUT In this chapter, Paul continues his defense of himself to some of the rebellious group of Corinthian believers who were refusing the authority of his ministry among them. He told them in verse 14 that he was ready to come to them for the _____ time. What three things did he say distinguished or marked a true apostle (v. 12)? (1) _____, (2) _____ and (3) _____

MAKE YOUR CHOICE Who do I know that looks up to me as an example? _____ How can I be a more godly leader to them?
_____

SATURDAY · 2 Corinthians 13:1-14

TAKE THE CHALLENGE How do you do on tests at school? Do you like to take tests?

CHECK IT OUT Paul tells us in verse 5 to

"_____ yourselves"

to make sure you are in the

_____.

In other words, make sure you know you

are truly a Christian — that your faith is real.

MAKE YOUR CHOICE Write down three proofs that show you truly know Christ as your personal Savior: (1) _____, (2)_____, (3) _____
If you're not sure of your faith, talk to a godly believer today and find out how to make sure.

christ your crs

Is evolution real or a myth?

Check it out this week to see The Creator of the Universe do His thing! It's no monkey business!

Sunday   Genesis 1:1-19

TAKE THE CHALLENGE

Have you ever looked at the stars and wondered what the world was like up there?

CHECK IT OUT

Imagine total darkness and then...

from nothing ...everything! What

does the Bible say that God created on

day 1:_____

day 2:_____

day 3:_____

day 4:_____

MAKE YOUR CHOICE

The Great Creator of the Universe loves me and created this world for me. If you know Jesus, read Ephesians 1:4 to find out how long God has loved you and wanted you for His own. Write it here:

_____

monday

Genesis 1:20-2:3

TAKE THE CHALLENGE

What would it be like to be omnipotent?

CHECK IT OUT

Omnipotent means "all powerful." This is how powerful God is. He shows this in His Creation of the world! What did God create on day 5?

_____

On day 6? _____

On day 7 God _____ .

MAKE YOUR CHOICE

How does it make me feel to know that God is omnipotent? _____ What are some things God can do because of His omnipotence that humans can't do? _____

Tuesday

Genesis 2:4-25

TAKE THE CHALLENGE

The human race begins in today's passage!

CHECK IT OUT

Eden was an awesome place! It wasn't just a big vegetable garden! Check out the following verses and see what else was in this awesome garden!

Verse 9 – **t**_____   Verse 10 – **r**_____

Verse 11 – **g**_____   Verse 12 – **o**_____

Verse 15 – **m**_____   Verse 19 – **b**_____

and **b**_____   v. 22 – **w**_____

MAKE YOUR CHOICE

God made the earth in six days, but Jesus has had thousands of years to prepare my home in Heaven! What will I love most about the place that Jesus is creating for me? _____ What do I love about earth that I can praise God for right now? _____

51

wednesday — Genesis 3:1-19

TAKE THE CHALLENGE

Paradise... LOST!

CHECK IT OUT

Imagine that you are rich, living in a mansion with your every need supplied, and that you even have a loving family. All of a sudden, you are on the street on your own, dirty and hungry, with no money. This was Adam and Eve's reality. What choices did they make to cause this? _____ Who appears for the first time in verse 1?_____ What did he try to get the woman to do?_____

What were the consequences of their sin?_____

_____

What is something bad that has happened to me when I chose to disobey God and sin?_____
Does sin always have consequences? _____ Who loves me but hates my sin?_____ Sin separates me from whom? Why?_____

Thursday — Genesis 3:20-4:12

TAKE THE CHALLENGE

CSI - Genesis

CHECK IT OUT

Pretend you are on the case of Abel's murder and answer these questions from today's passage.

Who killed Abel?_____

What was his relationship to the victim?_____

What was his motive for killing him?_____

What was his punishment for the murder he committed?

_____

Cain and Abel were supposed to love and respect each other... They were family! How do I get along with my family?_____
Do I treat my parents and siblings with the respect and love they deserve?_____ I will take time now to write a note of love and appreciation to someone in my house.

FRIDAY   Genesis 4:25-5:14

TAKE THE CHALLENGE

Can you do the math?

CHECK IT OUT

How old was Adam when Seth was born?_____

How old was Adam when he died?_____ How old

was Seth when Enos(h) was born?_____ How old

was Seth when he died? _____ How old was

Enos(h) when he died?_____ Yikes! People lived a

LONG time back in Adam's day. What do you think

it would be like to live that long?_____

_____

I don't know how long my life will be. I need to ask God to
help me live my life to please Him every day. I can please
God today by:_____

SATURDAY   Genesis 5:15-32

Missing... without a trace! ...Enoch!

TAKE THE CHALLENGE

CHECK IT OUT

What happened to Enoch (v. 24)? _____

_____

Why do you think God took him? _____

_____

What do you think Enoch's family thought when he was

gone?_____

Enoch was obviously very close to the heart of God. What
are some ways that I can grow closer to God?_____

_____

53

christy rogers

Extra! Extra! Read all about it!

Flood destroys earth... Eight humans survive with boat of animals! Tower almost to sky... strange phenomenon mixes languages! Is it aliens?!? No, it's Almighty God!

Sunday — Genesis 6:1-16

TAKE THE CHALLENGE

A biography of a boat builder!

CHECK IT OUT

Noah was a man who knew and loved God. This was amazing considering he didn't have the Bible to read like we do today. What can you find out about Noah in today's passage? Noah was _____ and _____ (v. 9). Noah w _ _ _ _ _ with G _ _. Noah had three sons, S _ _ _, H _ _ and J _ _ _ _ _ _. What did God tell Noah to do in verse 14?_____ Why was he going to do this (v.13)?_____

MAKE YOUR CHOICE

Sin is everywhere: bad language at school...wrong images on TV and in magazines...fights among friends and in families. What can I do to protect my mind from the sin all around me?_____
What should I do when I sin?_____

monday
Genesis 6:17-7:10

TAKE THE CHALLENGE   Git 'er done!

CHECK IT OUT — God gave Noah specific instructions how to make the ark, as well as what and whom to take with him in the ark. Pretend that you are an architect. Draw a picture of the ark using the direction that God gave Noah in verses 14-16. How many floors would it have? How long and how wide would it be? How many doors and windows would it have?

MAKE YOUR CHOICE   Noah didn't question God's instructions, even though there were no floodwaters or rain clouds in sight. Who has God set up in authority over me? _____ _____ Am I always quick to do what these people ask of me?_____ How can I do better at obeying God and these people?

Tuesday
Genesis 7:11-24

TAKE THE CHALLENGE   God predicts 40 days and 40 nights of rain... and it happened!

CHECK IT OUT — Use the code to find the secret message of what happened to the earth when it rained.

1-A 2-D 3-E 4-G 5-H 6-I 7-L 8-N 9-O 10-P 11-R 12-S
13-T 14-U 15-V 16-W 17-Y

___ ___ ___ ___ ___   ___ ___ ___ ___ ___   ___ ___ ___ ___ ___
3 15 3 11 17   7   6 15   8   4   13   5   6   8   4

___ ___ ___   ___ ___ ___ ___ ___   ___ ___ ___
16 1 12   16   6 10   3   2   9 14   3

MAKE YOUR CHOICE   Am I glad that God gave me a way to be forgiven for my sin? _____ Do I praise Him for that?_____ How can I show God's love to my friend, _____ today?_____

55

wednesday
Genesis 8:1-12

TAKE THE CHALLENGE

The birds will know!

CHECK IT OUT

Aren't animals amazing? Noah used two kinds of birds to help him to be able to tell when the earth was dry. What were the two birds that helped him? A _____ and a _____.
What did one bird bring back that helped him know that the water was going down? _____
_____

MAKE YOUR CHOICE

The sun was shining and the earth was drying out. Noah and his family must have been pretty excited and hopeful. What gives me hope when I am facing a hard or scary situation? _____ Who do I talk to when I am discouraged or fearful? _____

Thursday
Genesis 8:13-22

TAKE THE CHALLENGE

Let's get out of here!

CHECK IT OUT

After so many months on the ark, Noah and his family must've been anxious to get onto dry land and walk around. How did they know it was time to get off the ark (v. 14)? _____ _____
What did Noah do when he finally got off the ark (v. 20)? _____ What did the Lord say in His heart after smelling Noah's sacrifice (v. 21)? _____

MAKE YOUR CHOICE

Noah's sacrifice was pleasing to God. What sacrifices could I make that would please God? _____ _____

FRIDAY   Genesis 9:1-19

TAKE THE CHALLENGE

CHECK IT OUT

Somewhere over the rainbow... God is Faithful!

A sign of the covenant that God made with Noah was a rainbow. What did God promise to Noah (and all people) with the sign of the rainbow?

_____

_____

Color in the rainbow.

MAKE YOUR CHOICE

What do I think of when I see a rainbow in the sky? Do I remember the faithfulness of God? **Yes / No** Who in my life has shown me what faithfulness looks like? _____
I will take time now and thank God for these faithful people.

SATURDAY   Genesis 11:1-9

TAKE THE CHALLENGE

CHECK IT OUT

This isn't a Lego® tower!

Have you ever tried to build a tower of blocks or Legos®? How far did you get? The people of Babel thought they could reach heaven by building a tower of bricks. They became proud and self-reliant. What did all the people of the world have in common in verse 1?_____ What did God do to confuse them and cause them to remember that they needed Him in verse 7?_____

MAKE YOUR CHOICE

The people of Babel constructed the tower as a monument to themselves and how great they were. What do I use in my life to tell others that I am cool? Circle answers. Popularity - humor music - sports - education - things - clothes - friends - money

Genesis 12:1-22:18

chrty rcrs

Get up and Go!

Take everything you have and move to a place that you have never seen!

This week we meet Abram . . . a man that God sent on an amazing journey! . . . Dive in!

Sunday Genesis 12:1-20

Liar, liar, pants on fire!

CHECK IT OUT

Abram and Sarai set out for Canaan, the land where God had sent them. After they had lived there awhile, there was a famine so they went to Egypt. There, Abram got himself in trouble with a lie that he told. What did he lie about?_____
Why?_____ What happened to the Egyptians because of his lie? _____
What do you think the Egyptians thought about Abram after this?_____

MAKE YOUR CHOICE

Am I a truthful person?_____ When my parents or teachers ask me things, do I ALWAYS tell the truth? _____ Right now I need to confess to God the sin of:

monday

Genesis 13:1-18

TAKE THE CHALLENGE — Fight, fight, fight!

CHECK IT OUT — Abram and his nephew, Lot, had both acquired much livestock by this time. They both had herdsmen working for them. What was happening between the herdsmen in verse 7?_____

What was the solution that Abram came up with in verse 9?_____ Which part did Lot choose in verse 10?_____Why?_____
_____ What sinful cities were near the portion that Lot chose?_____

MAKE YOUR CHOICE — Abram let Lot choose first and put his nephew's desires ahead of his own. How often do I put others first?_____
What is a way that I can be unselfish today?_____

Tuesday

Genesis 14:12-24

TAKE THE CHALLENGE — What a crazy name!

CHECK IT OUT — Put the events in today's passage in the order they occurred:

___ Abram gives 10% of everything to Melchizedek.
___ Lot is captured in a war.
___ Abram gathers his men.
___ Abram hears about Lot's plight.
___ Abram defeats the enemy and saves Lot.
___ Abram refuses to accept the goods of the King of Sodom.

MAKE YOUR CHOICE — Melchizedek was the priest of God at the time of Abram. Abram showed his respect and reverence for God by giving a tithe of his riches to God. How or what can I give to God? _____
_____ I will give $_____ this week!

wednesday Genesis 15:1-18

TAKE THE CHALLENGE
What a strange way to make a promise!

CHECK IT OUT

Today's passage talks about God's covenant (or promise) to Abram. What was the promise that God made to Abram?_____

What were the animals that God asked Abram to bring for the sacrifice? h_____ g_____
r_____ turtle d_____ young p_____

What did he do with the animals? _____

What happened as the sun set?_____

As the LORD sealed His covenant with Abram, He promised his desendants all the land between the Nile River and the E_____ River.

MAKE YOUR CHOICE

God's promise to Abram was fulfilled. God always keeps His promises! A promise I can claim today, if I know Jesus, is found in Hebrews 13:5b. Write it here: _____
_____

Thursday Genesis 17:1-8, 15-19

TAKE THE CHALLENGE
Are you kidding, Lord?

CHECK IT OUT

God again renews His promise to give Abraham a son... and Abraham is 100 years old!
Search for the words and names from today's passage. (Notice that God changed Abram & Sarai's names!)

```
L T U B L E S S I N G
E G W I P O B V D P A
A T S A R A H L Y E B
M J O F U K W Q L D R
H T N H P O B V D K A
S Y F I K M A Q N U H
I S A A C O B V D W A
A R E T H G U A L R M
```

Abraham   **laughter**   **Sarah**   **old**
Isaac   **blessing**   **Ishmael**   **son**

MAKE YOUR CHOICE

What is something amazing that God has done in my life or for me lately?_____

I will take the time right now to praise God for this!

FRIDAY   Genesis 18:1-14

The Promise, Part II

Three men came to Abraham and Sarah's house. How did they welcome these visitors? What did they do for the visitors in verse 2?_____ _____, verse 4?_____ _____ and in verse 5? _____ _____ What promise did they make about Sarah (v. 10)?_____ What did Sarah do when she heard it (v. 12)? _____

How do I treat guests in my home? (Circle any that may apply to you.) I retreat to my room and ignore them. I selfishly play my video/computer games and don't let others play. I keep all my toys off limits so that nothing gets broken. I am mean to kids that are younger than me. How SHOULD I treat them?_____

SATURDAY   Genesis 22:1-18

What is happening?

Abraham now has his beautiful son that God had promised to him, and then God asks Abraham to kill him! In a few sentences, write what happened to Abraham and Isaac on a mountain in the land of Moriah:

_____
_____
_____

Why do you think God asked Abraham to do this?_____
_____

What is something that God wants me to do that I think is hard? (some examples: witness to my friend at school, obey my parents without complaining, play with my younger brother or sister without fighting) _____
_____

61

chrtyrcrs

Would you marry someone you had never met? Isaac did, and his story is told here this week...

amazing!

Sunday   Genesis 24:1-15

TAKE THE CHALLENGE

The "prince" needs a wife!

CHECK IT OUT

Abraham is getting old and wants to find a bride for his son, Isaac. However, he doesn't want Isaac marrying a foreigner. He wants him to marry someone from his own people. So, a servant heads back to Abraham's home country. When he gets there.... To whom did the servant pray for guidance? _____ What would the girl do if she was the "right one"? _____
How soon did God answer the servant's prayer (v.15)?
_____

MAKE YOUR CHOICE

Prayer is so important! Take time right now to pray for:
-someone who needs to know Jesus   -someone who is sick
-someone who is sad   -someone in your family
-someone on the mission field   -someone who teaches you at
                                        your church

Monday

Genesis 24:16-33

The "princess" is found!

CHECK IT OUT

Color the sections of the picture that have a dot in them to find out what Rebekah showed to Abraham's servant.

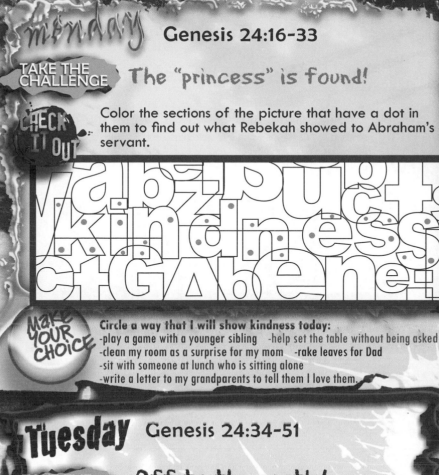

MAKE YOUR CHOICE

Circle a way that I will show kindness today:
-play a game with a younger sibling   -help set the table without being asked
-clean my room as a surprise for my mom   -rake leaves for Dad
-sit with someone at lunch who is sitting alone
-write a letter to my grandparents to tell them I love them.

Tuesday

Genesis 24:34-51

Off to the castle!

CHECK IT OUT

What does Rebekah's father say in verse 51 when the servant is done telling his story?

T_ _ _   H_ _   A_ _   G!

Why do you think he was able to say this? (Hint: see end of verse 51.) _____

Do you think Rebekah was a little scared to be leaving her home and family?_____

MAKE YOUR CHOICE

Someday God may ask me to go somewhere far away from my family. What do I need to remember when I am faced with a hard or scary situation? Write Philippians 4:13 here:" _____
_____

wednesday — Genesis 24:52-67

 Is it love at first sight?

 CHECK IT OUT

Today's passage is almost like a TV love story! Boy sees girl. Girl sees boy. Servant explains story. Boy marries girl. Did Isaac love Rebekah? Check verse 67 for the answer. _____

MAKE YOUR CHOICE

Now is not too early to start praying for God to guide you to the right person to marry. Some things to pray for might be: -someone who loves and knows Jesus -someone who is kind -someone who loves the Bible -someone who is not hot-tempered. I will pray for my future mate right now!

Thursday — Genesis 25:19-34

TAKE THE CHALLENGE A house divided.

CHECK IT OUT

Jacob and Rebekah had twins, but they were not identical. Their parents even played favorites! In the two houses below, write who each parent's favorite was and what the differences were between the brothers.

JACOB   REBEKAH

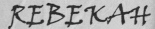

MAKE YOUR CHOICE

The Bible tells us not to compare ourselves with others. Each of us was created in a unique and special way. What is one thing about myself that I would like to change? _____
I will take time right now to thank God for making me who I am. I will remember that He loves me and made me special!

FRIDAY — Genesis 27:1-17

TAKE THE CHALLENGE

It's a plot!

CHECK IT OUT

Today's passage sounds like a criminal plot! What two people were making a plan?_____ and _____ Whom were they trying to deceive? _____ Whom were they trying to cheat?_____ What were they trying to steal?_____

MAKE YOUR CHOICE

Deceiving people always leads to hurt feelings and lack of trust. Have I told a lie recently?_____ Have I exaggerated the truth to make myself look better?_____ How does God feel about deceit and truthfulness? Look up Proverbs 12:22.

SATURDAY — Genesis 27:18-33

TAKE THE CHALLENGE

It's a case of mistaken identity!

CHECK IT OUT

Isaac gives his blessing...but not to the firstborn Esau! Jacob and Rebekah deceive him into THINKING that he is blessing Esau. What does Isaac ask for Jacob in his blessing? In verse 28 about food and riches?_____ In verse 29a about foreign nations? _____ In verse 29b about those who bless and curse him?_____ Would Jacob have been blessed anyway, without his and his mother's plot? See Gen. 25:23._____

MAKE YOUR CHOICE

God's timing is always best, even when it seems like waiting is hard. What is something that I have had a hard time waiting for?_____ Can I see how God's timing was best for me?_____

Genesis 27:34-35:15

As we continue the story of Abraham's family tree, let's review where we've been in the Middle East so far in Genesis.

Can you find these places? <u>The Mountains of Ararat</u> (Noah), <u>Babel</u> (tower of languages), <u>Ur</u> (Abraham's birthplace), <u>Haran</u> (where Abraham and Lot settled for awhile), <u>Shechem</u> (where Abraham and Sarai settled in the Promised Land), <u>Hebron</u> (where Abraham, Isaac, and Jacob all lived and were buried), <u>Beer-Sheba</u> (where Isaac received God's covenant), and <u>Bethel</u>, where we'll find Jacob in this week's scripture.

Sunday — Genesis 27:34-45

TAKE THE CHALLENGE

Is it ever right to do wrong in order to try to make things work out right?

CHECK IT OUT

Put the names of the people in this passage beside the thing they did or said that was not good — even though maybe they were trying to change things for the better.

_____ Told Esau that one day he would get the best of his younger brother.

_____ Sent her youngest son away to Haran to escape his brother's anger.

_____ Deceitfully stole his older brother's blessing.

_____ Wanted to kill his younger brother after his father died.

Names to choose from: Rebekah, Jacob, Isaac, Esau

MAKE YOUR CHOICE

Will getting angry at someone who has been unfair to me, and wanting to hurt them, help the situation or hurt it? _____

Why? _____

God wants me to _____ my enemies.

Genesis 28:10-22

TAKE THE CHALLENGE

Where were you when you came to know Jesus personally as your Savior?

HEAVEN

CHECK IT OUT

Jacob is at a very important place in his life in this chapter. He later names it _____ (verse 19), meaning "House of God", because this is where he personally meets the Almighty God. On each rung of the "Ladder to Heaven", put one phrase from the great promises God made to him in verses 13-15.

MAKE YOUR CHOICE

I found Jesus as my Savior when I was at _____

_____.

I will thank Him today for the promise of eternal life in Him.

Tuesday   Genesis 29:1-20

TAKE THE CHALLENGE

Have you ever asked your Mother and Dad how they met and ended up marrying?

CHECK IT OUT

Here we have another love story! It's interesting that Jacob meets and falls in love with his bride at a _____ just like his father and mother had done. His uncle Laban was his mom's brother (v. 13). Notice how gracious his uncle was (vv. 13-16): He _____ to meet him. He _____ and _____ him. He brought him to his _____. He let Jacob stay with him for a whole _____. He offered to _____ Jacob for his work. What did Jacob ask for as pay (v. 18)? _____ as his wife

MAKE YOUR CHOICE

What would be most important to me in choosing a mate someday? _____ I will begin praying today that God will help me find HIS special person for me someday.

wednesday Genesis 31:3-18

TAKE THE CHALLENGE

Have you and your family ever had to move to a new state? What was the hardest thing for you when you left your old home?

CHECK IT OUT

How did God identify Himself in verse 13? "I am
_____ _____ ___ _____" He
reminded Jacob that he had made a _____
to Him there. What hard thing was He asking Jacob and his
family to do now? (1) To _____
and to (2) _____
Jacob (circle one) **obeyed God and moved** / **disobeyed
and stayed where he was in Haran.**

MAKE YOUR CHOICE

What's the hardest thing God has asked me to do? _____
_____ Did I obey or disobey?
_____What will I do next time God calls me to do
something hard? _____

Thursday Genesis 32:1-12

TAKE THE CHALLENGE

When was the last time you ran into an angel? In the Bible, angels often appeared to people as men to guide and protect them.

CHECK IT OUT

Who would Jacob have to straighten things out with and
seek forgiveness if he was to return to his "native land" of
Israel? _____, his brother What did Jacob call
the place where God's angels met him to help him with this meeting?
_____ This word literally meant "two camps." Jacob
went to meet Esau in two groups or camps. How many men were
coming with Esau (v. 6)? _____

MAKE YOUR CHOICE

God has guardian _____ to protect and care for
me, too. What dangerous things do I face everyday that I
never stop to think about? _____
_____

68

FRIDAY

Genesis 32:13-20

TAKE THE CHALLENGE

If your brother had wanted to kill you the last time you had seen him, what do you think you would give him to get him to make up with you?

CHECK IT OUT

Check out Jacob's gifts to Esau, his estranged brother. Circle the gifts in the word search on the right.

goats (2x), ewes, rams, camels, colts, kine, cows, bulls, donkeys (2x), asses

```
R T U B U L L S S N S
A G W E N I K V T P Y
M T S A R A O L A S E
S S E S S A S O O T K
T E W E S O B W G L N
A Y F I K L M A O O O
O S A A S L E M A C D
G R E T D O N K E Y S
```

MAKE YOUR CHOICE

Do you think Jacob was up to his old tricks again, coming up with a plan to save his own skin? _____ How often do I think up some big plan instead of asking for God's help? _____ Why can I always trust God? _____

SATURDAY

Genesis 35:9-15

TAKE THE CHALLENGE

Have you ever wished you could change your name? What would you like to change it to?

CHECK IT OUT

Verse 9 tells us that God appeared again to Jacob after he left the place called Padan-aram. God b_____ him here and then in verse 10 He changed his name from _____ to _____. "Jacob" meant, "he deceives" or "holding the heel" and "Israel" meant, "he struggles with God." Back in chapter 32, Jacob had actually wrestled with God, given in to Him, and allowed Him to take control of his life. What did God call Himself here in verse 11: "I am _____ _____." What command did He give Jacob in this same verse? "Be _____ and _____."

MAKE YOUR CHOICE

Just like God told Jacob — now named "Israel" — to "be fruitful" for Him, so Christ told believers the same thing: "to bear fruit." When others look at my life, what kind of fruit do they see me producing for God? _____

14

WEEKLY PASSAGES COVERED

Genesis 37:1-41:36

As we begin a new section of Genesis – the Joseph Narratives – we will see many parallels between Joseph and Jesus. To begin with, Joseph is the only Old Testament character that has no sin recorded about him. Of course, we know that JESUS was the only truly sinless Man ever to walk this earth. We will also see that Joseph was highly favored by his father just as Jesus was God's very special Son. Keep your eyes on the parallels as you follow Joseph's life. You will be amazed!

JESUS

JOSEPH

Sunday — Genesis 37:1-17

TAKE THE CHALLENGE

When was the last time you had a nightmare or weird dream? Do you remember your dreams when you wake up?

CHECK IT OUT

Jacob settled in (1 DOWN). His son, (2 ACROSS) was 17 years old. Jacob's new wives were: b(3 ACROSS) and z(4 DOWN). Jacob made his favored son a special c(1 ACROSS) (some translations refer to it as a tunic or robe). Joseph's brothers (5 DOWN) him. Joseph dreamed about (6 DOWN) of grain in a field bowing down to him. He also dreamed of the sun, moon and (7 DOWN) stars bowing to him. The brothers took the flocks of sheep down to (6 ACROSS). Joseph finally found them in (8 DOWN). His brothers plotted to (9 DOWN) him.

CANAAN, JOSEPH, BILHAH, ZILPAH, COAT, HATED, SHEAVES, ELEVEN, SHECHEM, DOTHAN

MAKE YOUR CHOICE

What did I learn from this true story of Joseph about what NOT to do to make my brothers and sisters feel badly? _____

What can I do to encourage my brothers or sisters? _____

Genesis 37:18-36

TAKE THE CHALLENGE

As you read the next part of the Joseph story today, can you see any ways his story was like Jesus' life?

CHECK IT OUT

What did Joseph's brothers plot to do to him? _____ _____Who kept them from going through with their plan? _____ What did he plan to do later (v. 22b)? _____

But instead, what happened to Joseph after being put in the pit or cistern? _____

How much was he sold for? _____ pieces or shekels of _____

What did Jacob believe had happened to his son (v. 33)? _____

_____

MAKE YOUR CHOICE

Would I have been more like Reuben or the other brothers in this story? _____ What kind thing can I do for my annoying brother or sister today to let them know I do love them? _____

Tuesday Genesis 39:1-16

TAKE THE CHALLENGE

What's the first thing you should do when you're in a place where you are being tempted to sin?

CHECK IT OUT

After being taken to Egypt as a slave, Joseph finds himself working for a very important soldier in Egypt's army named: _____. Two times in verses two and three, it says "the _____ was _____ him (Joseph)." Because God blessed and prospered him, he became the _____ of everything in Potiphar's house. But who tried to tempt him to sin and then falsely accused him of sexual misconduct? _____

MAKE YOUR CHOICE

Can you think of who tried to tempt the Lord Jesus to sin in the New Testament? _____ When Joseph was tempted, what did he do (See verse 12.)? _____
What is the first thing I should do when I'm in a place of temptation to sin? ____ _____ _____ !!!

wednesday — Genesis 39:17-40:8

TAKE THE CHALLENGE

How'd you like to end up in prison for doing the RIGHT thing?? Check out what happened to poor Joseph in today's passage

CHECK IT OUT

Even when Joseph was thrown in the king's _____ _____ for something he didn't even do, God worked in the prison _____'s heart to like Joseph and show (extend to) him _____.

Two times again in this passage (verses 21 and 23) we read again that "the _____ was _____ him (Joseph)." Who did God use Joseph to encourage in the prison? A _____ and a _____

MAKE YOUR CHOICE

Even in the worst situations or conditions, God will be _____ me always. And there will always be someone I can encourage. Who do I know who is going through a tough time today? _____ What could I do to encourage them? _____

Thursday — Genesis 40:9-23

TAKE THE CHALLENGE

Have you discovered any of your spiritual gifts yet? You DO have one! Start asking God to show you what it is!

CHECK IT OUT

God had given Joseph the amazing ability to interpret others' _____. Do the matching game below to see how much you learned from this true story.

_____ 1. Joseph
_____ 2. The chief butler (or cupbearer)
_____ 3. A 3-branched grape vine that produced wine
_____ 4. The chief baker
_____ 5. 3 baskets of bread with birds eating out of the top

A. Dreamed of bread baskets
B. Meant in 3 days, Pharaoh would restore him to his position
C. Gifted by God to interpret dreams
D. Dreamed of a productive grape vine
E. Meant he would be killed by hanging

MAKE YOUR CHOICE

Something I can do to discover the spiritual gift God has given me as a Christian, is to get involved helping others in different ways and see how God uses me. What could I do this week to reach out and help someone or minister in my church? _____

FRIDAY
Genesis 41:1-16

TAKE THE CHALLENGE Did someone ever do something really nice for you, but you forgot to go back and thank them?

CHECK IT OUT Who had two very strange dreams in today's passage? _____ His first dream was about _____ and his second was about _____ . In both cases, the (circle one) thin / fat ate up the (circle one) **thin** / **fat.** Who remembered to finally tell Pharaoh about Joseph's interpreting abilities? The _____ When Joseph was called before Pharaoh, who did he give the credit to for his ability to interpret dreams? ___ ___ ___

MAKE YOUR CHOICE When I accomplish something really good in my life, do I take the credit for myself or give it to GOD who gave me my abilities and gifts? _____ When someone compliments or praises me, how can I give the credit to God? _____
_____

SATURDAY
Genesis 41:17-36

TAKE THE CHALLENGE Sometimes, as we let God use us to do small things, He takes what we did and gives us the chance to do something really big — maybe even for our whole nation! Check out Joseph's story today.

CHECK IT OUT Joseph said the seven fat cows and full heads of grain in Pharaoh's dreams symbolized seven good, abundant years. But the seven _____ cows and _____ _____ heads of grain symbolized seven years of severe _____. This means no food would grow! Joseph's dream interpretation helped Pharaoh to accept and put into motion Joseph's plan to put food in reserve for the famine that was coming.

MAKE YOUR CHOICE I will do what God has called me to do NOW, and one day He may use me to be a major influence in my community, state or country! What are some things I'd be willing to do someday for God — with His help? _____ _____

WEEKLY PASSAGES COVERED
Genesis 41:37-44:34

chrtyyrcrs

Did you know that archaeology backs up the Genesis account of the Egyptian famine? One document from 100 B.C. actually describes a seven-year famine in the days of Zoser of the Third Dynasty (2700 B.C.). The titles of "chief of the butlers" and "chief of the bakers" is also mentioned in these documents.

Sunday — Genesis 41:37-57

TAKE THE CHALLENGE

Have you ever won a special award at school or a medal at Olympian Club? How does it make you feel to be called up and rewarded in front of everyone?

CHECK IT OUT

Circle the things that the Pharaoh did for Joseph because of his godly character:

Made him ruler of everything

Gave him his special ring   Gave him his favorite dogs

Dressed him in kingly robes   Put a toe ring on his big toe

Placed a gold chain around his neck

Gave him a really cool bicycle   Made him the garbage collector

Gave him a chariot to ride around the land

How old was Joseph when he began to collect and store all the food for Egyapt's approaching famine years? _____ years old He had two sons whom he named _____ and _____.

MAKE YOUR CHOICE

What would I most like to be rewarded for in the coming year? _____

_____ I will work my hardest with God's help to be the best I can be!

monday
Genesis 42:1-20

TAKE THE CHALLENGE
Can you imagine not seeing your parents or brothers and sisters for over 20 years? Do you think you'd still recognize them?

CHECK IT OUT

When _____ learned there was grain in _____, he sent _____ of his sons down to buy some. How did Joseph's dreams as a teenager come true here in verse 6? _____ _____ Joseph _____ them but they did NOT _____ him. Joseph wanted them to bring back their _____ brother, the one he had been closest to.

MAKE YOUR CHOICE

Joseph could have put all his brothers in prison and kept them there, after what they had done to him. - God wants me to f_____ people when they hurt me. Jesus showed us how when he _____ on the cross for us, his enemies. (Try memorizing Ephesians 4:32 to help you with this!)

Tuesday
Genesis 42:21-38

TAKE THE CHALLENGE
Even though Joseph knew what he was doing, the brothers and his father had no idea and were so afraid that they would lose more lives. What makes you feel afraid?

CHECK IT OUT

Joseph ended up keeping S_____ as ransom for the brothers. He also secretly put the _____ coins they had used to pay for their grain back in their _____. He even _____ when they weren't looking (v. 24). How did elderly Jacob respond when the nine brothers returned and told him the whole story of what had happened? _____ _____ He swore that he could not send his youngest _____, because losing him would kill him.

MAKE YOUR CHOICE

Just as Joseph knew what he was doing, sometimes I may feel like everything is going wrong, but forget that GOD knows what He is doing in my life. What is a hard situation or trial that I'm having to deal with right now? _____
How might God want to make me a better person through this hardship? _____

wednesday — Genesis 43:1-15

TAKE THE CHALLENGE

How am I training to be a leader? Do I lead others to be more Christ-like?

CHECK IT OUT

Which brother took the lead here when they needed to get more grain? _____ He talked his father, Jacob, into sending their _____ _____ along. (His name was _____ (v. 15). This was the only way to keep the whole family from _____. List some of the Israelite gifts Jacob sent with the brothers to the Egyptian man (actually Joseph!) to win his favor (vv. 11-12). _____ _____ _____ _____ _____ _____ _____

MAKE YOUR CHOICE

Name three kind things Joseph did for his brothers, especially Benjamin, in this account: (1) _____
(2) _____ (3) _____
How do you know that this whole incident was very touching for Joseph? (See verse 30.) _____

Thursday — Genesis 43:16-34

TAKE THE CHALLENGE

How can I be kind to someone who has wronged or hurt me in the past? See how Joseph did this in today's account.

CHECK IT OUT

Name three kind things Joseph did for his brothers, especially Bejamin, in this account: 1) _____

2) _____ 3) _____

How do you know that this whole incident was very touching for Joseph? (See verse 30.) _____

_____

MAKE YOUR CHOICE

How can I follow Joseph's wonderful example of forgiveness and love in this passage?

_____

FRIDAY   Genesis 44:1-17

Were you ever accused of doing something you didn't do? Not a fun thing is it?

CHECK IT OUT

What did Joseph place in Benjamin's sack of grain? His own _____ _____ When the cup was found in Benjamin's sack, who took leadership and stood up for him? _____ He said they would stay there as Joseph's _____ (v. 16b) until the issue could be resolved. He refused to leave Benjamin there alone.

MAKE YOUR CHOICE

What did Jesus Christ do when he was wrongly accused and sentenced to death on a cross? _____ (The gospel accounts tell us "He opened not His mouth.") Sometimes it's better not to defend myself with words, but to just prove I'm innocent by my Christ-like actions. What about Jesus would I like someone to see in my life today? _____

SATURDAY   Genesis 44:18-34

TAKE THE CHALLENGE

Sometimes taking leadership means stepping up and having to make special sacrifices.

CHECK IT OUT

Who again takes full leadership here? _____ After he recounts the whole story for Joseph, he offers himself as Joseph's slave in place of _____. He begs Joseph to let Benjamin return home to their father so that he won't _____ from grief.

MAKE YOUR CHOICE

Am I willing to be a leader even when it hurts me sometimes? Yes/ No
What sacrifices might I have to make in order to lead others in the way of goodness and peace? _____
How do I show concern for my father like Judah did? _____
_____

77

As we come to the completion of the Joseph narratives, here are a couple of interesting facts you may not have known!

~ *Joseph's special coat was a source of irritation to his hard-working brothers, as it had long sleeves. People who had to do hard work wore short sleeves!*

~ *The pyramids had been standing for 1000 years when Joseph arrived in Egypt!*

~ *Egyptian men shaved their beards, and wore ornate headpieces, jewelry, and make-up – yes, MAKE-UP! No wonder Joseph's brothers didn't recognize him!*

Sunday   Genesis 45:1-15

TAKE THE CHALLENGE

Family Reunions! Such great times to get together and have fun with uncles, aunts and cousins you haven't seen in awhile! Read about Joseph's family reunion today!

TRUE or FALSE:

CHECK IT OUT

_____ Joseph could not control his weeping because he was so emotional!

_____ Joseph invited all his servants and helpers in to see his reunion with his brothers.

_____ Joseph's brothers were all excited and full of joy when he said who he was.

_____ After going back through his whole story, Joseph concluded that it was not THEY (the brothers) who had sent him to Egypt, but GOD.

_____ Joseph hugged his brother Reuben first of all, weeping over him.

_____ Joseph asked the brothers to bring his father down to be with him as quickly as possible.

MAKE YOUR CHOICE

Look back again at verse 8. What is God doing in my life right now that I can't really understand yet? _____ Can I trust that HE is in control and will do His will in and through me?

Yes / No

monday

Genesis 45:16-28

TAKE THE CHALLENGE

What do you and your siblings (brothers or sisters) argue about the most?

CHECK IT OUT

In today's account we see _____ (v. 16) rejoicing with Joseph about his family reunion. He invites all of them to move to _____ and enjoy (eat) "the _____ of the _____." This means they were going to be very well taken care of! Old _____ would be so thrilled to find out his _____ was still alive and that he was the _____ _____ over all Egypt! - But notice the last thing Joseph said (v. 24) to all his brothers before they left to get their father and bring him back: "_____ _____." Why do you think he felt it necessary to warn his brothers not to fight or argue on the way back? _____ What might they argue about? _____

MAKE YOUR CHOICE

Sometimes I argue with my brother or sister — or my friend. How can I be more thoughtful of their feelings instead of thinking of myself first? _____

Tuesday

Genesis 46:1-7; 28-30

TAKE THE CHALLENGE

Can you imagine making a big move to another country if you were over 100 years old? That would really be a tough move, wouldn't it?

CHECK IT OUT

Do you like math class? Let's do some math today! We're going to see how many Israelites ended up moving to Egypt in all:

Leah's children & grands (v. 15)	**33**
Zilpah's children & grands (v. 18)	**16**
Rachel's children & grands (v. 22)	**14**
Bilhah's children & grands (v. 25)	**+ 7**

Now take a peek at Exodus 1:6-7 to see what happened to them there. Had Jacob succeeded in being "fruitful"? **Yes / No**

TOTAL _____

MAKE YOUR CHOICE

Look at verse 4. Whenever God asks me to do something, whether easy or difficult, _____ will go WITH me!

wednesday — Genesis 47:1-12, 27-31

TAKE THE CHALLENGE

Have you and your family ever had to move to another whole state or country because you could find no food to eat where you lived?

CHECK IT OUT

Today we see Joseph and _____ of his brothers going to ask _____ if he could give them a place to live. What question did Pharaoh ask them in verse 3: "What is _____ _____?" They told him that they were _____ and that their flocks of sheep had no _____. Pharaoh gave them the (circle one) - worst, best, ugliest — piece of property to live on. The name of the land was _____. How old was Joseph's daddy when he introduced him to Pharaoh here? _____

MAKE YOUR CHOICE

Did God take care of Joseph's family? Yes / No

What's one way God has taken care of YOU this week?

_____

Thursday — Genesis 48:1-16

TAKE THE CHALLENGE

Have you ever had your grandfather or uncle or maybe your pastor put his hand on your head and compliment, bless, or pray for you?

CHECK IT OUT

When Joseph heard that his father was very ill, he took his two sons, _____ and _____ with him to see their grandfather before he died. Israel (Jacob) said that God _____ had appeared to him and promised that He was going to make Joseph's family a _____ of people (v.4) Then Israel took his grandsons up on his lap and blessed them. He put his right hand on _____'s head and his left hand on _____'s head. Who was the oldest son? _____

Who should have received the right-handed (best) blessing? _____

Does this remind you of something that happened to Jacob and Esau way back when they were blessed by Abraham?

MAKE YOUR CHOICE

Is there a godly relative or leader at my church I could ask to pray for me, that I'll grow up to be a godly person. Somebody I look up to and could ask to do this is: _____ (their name). Now call or write and ASK them!

Genesis 49:8-10,22-28

TAKE THE CHALLENGE

Isn't it interesting that in most families every child is very different?

CHECK IT OUT

Skim through the verses to see what Jacob's blessings and future predictions were for each of his sons. You can tell they were all very different from each other. Match the son to the picture that best shows his blessing.

Reuben, Simeon & Levi, Judah, Zebulun,

Issachar, Dan, Gad, Asher, Naphtali, Joseph, Benjamin

Make YOUR CHOICE

Isn't it neat that God makes all of us so different? What symbol would my parents probably use to describe ME if they were going to picture the kind of person I am?

_____

SATURDAY

Genesis 50:7-26

TAKE THE CHALLENGE

If you were about to die, what would you want to tell those you love the most?

CHECK IT OUT

What two people do we see that died in this passage (vv. 7, 26)? _____ and _____

Jacob was 147 when he died. How old was Joseph? _____ What did Joseph assure his brothers in verses 20 and 21? Write both sentences out on the lines:

" _____

_____ "

Make YOUR CHOICE

The whole focus of Joseph's life is found in his wonderful statement in verse 20. When people mean harm to me and are unkind, _____ will use it for _____ to accomplish HIS purpose in my life and promote my spiritual growth! Write down one hard thing God has used to make you a better person: _____

81

Matthew 1:1–4:25

Have you ever wondered what happened between the Old and New Testaments and how long it was?

Well, actually, the books of Ezra, Nehemiah, and Esther tell us what happened in the last 100 years of Old Testament history. Malachi was the last of the Old Testament prophets. After his book was written, 400 years passed before Jesus' birth! Those years are often called "the years of silence." During this time, Palestine was conquered and ruled by the Greeks and later the Romans.

Sunday — Matthew 1:1-17

TAKE THE CHALLENGE

Have you ever seen the "Family Tree" of your own family name? Well here in Matthew I, we see the family tree – or genealogy of Jesus' earthly stepfather, Joseph. (Remember that His REAL Father was God!)

CHECK IT OUT

Can you pick out 12 names from Joseph's genealogy in the Word Search? Circle them.

ABRAHAM	PEREZ	RAM
SALMON	OBED	BOAZ
DAVID	SOLOMON	ASA
UZZIAH	JOSIAH	ABIHUD
AZOR	ZADOK	JACOB

```
U Z Z I A H A I S O J
E E A D P M B V J B A
N R D A R A I L A E B
O E O V U R H O C D R
M P K I P O U B O K A
L D F D K L D M B R H
A B O A Z O R V D A A
S O L O M O N A S A M
```

MAKE YOUR CHOICE

Today I will thank God for the family He has given me. I will pray for those in my family who may not yet know Jesus as Savior. Write out your prayer here: _____

Matthew 1:18-25

TAKE THE CHALLENGE

Today you will read about a godly couple who loved their God more than each other.

CHECK IT OUT

What two people were engaged to be married here? _____ and _____
How did Mary get pregnant? By the _____ _____. Who came and told Joseph what was going on so he would not divorce his wife? An _____ of the _____ What were he and Mary to name this coming baby son? _____ All of this wonderful news fulfilled the Old Testament passage in Isaiah (7:14) that a _____ would be with _____.

MAKE YOUR CHOICE

"Jesus" means Jehovah saves! God sent Jesus down to earth as a baby to bring salvation to me! What did I need "saving" from? _____

Tuesday Matthew 2:1-12

TAKE THE CHALLENGE

Can you imagine very rich kings coming to your house and bringing you very expensive gifts?

CHECK IT OUT

Are these statements TRUE of FALSE? (Check the passage VERY CAREFULLY, as lots of things we've heard over the years about this story are not right!) _____ The wise men found Jesus in the town of Bethlehem, where the Old Testament scriptures had directed them. _____ There were only three wise men. _____ The wise men came from the far East — perhaps Persia. _____ There could have been a whole band (even dozens) of wise men accompanied by armed guards! _____ The wise men visited baby Jesus in the manger. _____ The wise men went back to see Herod after they had worshipped Jesus with their gifts. _____ The wise men gave Jesus gifts of gold, frankincense, and myrrh. HINT: Three of the above are false! Did you find them?

MAKE YOUR CHOICE

Many times I believe stories I read or hear without checking them out by the Word of God. I will always check the facts against _____'s _____ before I buy into them!!

wednesday — Matthew 2:13-23

TAKE THE CHALLENGE

Can you imagine having to run away from your house in the middle of the night because someone was trying to find and kill you?

CHECK IT OUT

Why did the angel tell Joseph in a dream that they needed to "Get up" and escape to _____?
_____

This would fulfill an Old Testament prophecy in Hosea 11:1, "Out of Egypt I have called my son." How very sad that _____ was so angry that the wise men didn't come back and tell him where Jesus was. He began to murder all little boys in Bethlehem who were _____ years old or under. (This also fulfilled a sad prophecy from the Old Testament, Jeremiah 31:15). After having the guiding help of two angel messages, Joseph left Egypt and finally ended up settling in what town? _____

MAKE YOUR CHOICE

Do you ever wish that angels would come and tell you just what to do? Well, guess what? Now I have God's Holy Word to guide me each day as I have my Quiet Time. Prayer: *"Thank You, Lord, for speaking to me through Your Holy Word. Help me to spend time with You each and every day!"*

Thursday — Matthew 3:1-17

TAKE THE CHALLENGE

Who do you know that likes to camp out all the time and hunt in the woods? Today we're going to meet a real outdoors man!

CHECK IT OUT

Who is introduced in this passage? _____ the _____ Describe this desert man's appearance and food choices: _____

He baptized people who were wanting to seek God with the water unto (for) r_____, but said One was coming who was _____ than he was, and that HE would baptize with the _____ _____ and _____. Then, Someone showed up at the _____ river, at just the right time to be introduced as God's Son from _____ : _____

MAKE YOUR CHOICE

What did God the Father call Jesus in verse 17 of today's passage? This is My
"_____" in (with) whom I am
"_____-_____." Is God pleased with me as His child?
He loves me as His own child and sent Jesus to live on earth and then die for my sins. I should be seeking to _____ Him everyday

FRIDAY   Matthew 4:1-11

TAKE THE CHALLENGE

When's the last time you were tempted to do something wrong? Who was with you?

CHECK IT OUT

Who was being tempted to sin in this account? _____ And who was the one doing the tempting? _____ Below are the three temptations he used to try to get Jesus to sin so he wouldn't be able to die for our sins. Number them in the order Satan presented them:

_____ Jump off the temple steeple!

_____ Bow down and worship me.

_____ Turn these stones into bread.

(Remember that Jesus hadn't eaten for _____ days!)

Who came and took care of Jesus after Satan gave up? The _____

MAKE YOUR CHOICE

When I am tempted, where should I turn for the strength I need to say "NO"? _____ (Hint: What did Jesus quote from each time he resisted Satan's attempts to get Him to sin? _____)

SATURDAY   Matthew 4:12-25

TAKE THE CHALLENGE

"I have decided to follow Jesus, . . . No turning back, no turning back." Have you ever sung that song at church? Today find four young men who did just that!

CHECK IT OUT

Jesus had gone to stay in the state of G_____ in a town by the lake (Sea of Galilee), in fulfillment of an Old Testament prophecy by Isaiah (9:1-2). He had begun to preach this message: "_____, for the _____ of _____ is at hand (near)!" By the Sea, Jesus called two sets of brothers to follow Him and be His disciples: S_____ P_____, A_____, J_____, J_____.

After calling these men to go with Him, He went all through Galilee doing three things (circle the right three): **Screaming Teaching Healing Baptizing Singing Preaching Proclaiming**

MAKE YOUR CHOICE

If Jesus were to see me at school or on the playground today, and call me to leave everything I'm used to and follow Him from now on, would I say "Yes" to the Savior or would I turn away? _____

WEEKLY PASSAGES COVERED
Matthew 5:1–7:29

ch rt yr crs

What are the GOSPELS?

There are four of them! They were written by four men: Matthew, Mark, Luke and John. The word "Gospel" means "good news!" They all share the "good news" about Jesus coming to earth to be our Savior. Matthew, Mark and Luke are called "synoptic Gospels" since they see and record Christ's life in the same way.

Sunday Matthew 5:1-16

TAKE THE CHALLENGE

Have you ever heard of the Beatitudes or maybe the "BE-ATTITUDES"? Check them out today!

CHECK IT OUT

When Jesus could have preached to crowds of people, He went instead up on a mountainside and taught just His disciples a lesson on the attitudes a follower of His should have. Can you match the BE-ATTITUDE with its result or reward below? **(Draw lines between them.)**

BE-ATTITUDE	RESULT or REWARD
• The poor in spirit	• They will be filled/satisfied
• Those who mourn (over their sin)	• They will see God
• The meek/gentle	• Theirs is the kingdom of heaven/ great reward (used twice)
• Those who hunger & thirst for righteousness	
• Those who are merciful	• They will be called sons/children of God
• The pure in heart	• They will be comforted
• The peacemakers	• They will inherit the earth
• Those who are persecuted for being right	• They shall obtain/receive mercy

MAKE YOUR CHOICE

These are all attitudes that Christ exhibited in HIS life! Circle the ones above that I need to pray for and work on with God's help.

Matthew 5:17-28

TAKE THE CHALLENGE

It's easy not to like rules, regulations, and laws, isn't it? Let's see what Jesus' attitude was toward God's rules?

CHECK IT OUT

In verse 17, Jesus says He did not come to _____ (do away with) the Law or the Prophets . . but to _____ them. He goes on later to say that whoever will _____ and _____ these commands will be called _____ in the kingdom of Heaven. Jesus says later that to HATE someone is just like _____ _____ them. Also, when a man looks at and thinks impure thoughts about a woman (sinful movies, pornography and sexual sites on the computer) just like the man committing _____ .

MAKE YOUR CHOICE

Jesus was and is concerned about sin in our lives! How concerned am I about the sinful habits or thoughts or actions in my own life? _____ Am I confessing my sins to Jesus each day and then turning from them? **Yes/ No**

Tuesday Matthew 5:33-48

TAKE THE CHALLENGE

Do you ever have to listen to others swear and take God's name in vain? Does it bother you when you hear that kind of language? What about on TV shows?

CHECK IT OUT

Jesus does some hard-hitting against three other important issues now: swearing, getting even against someone, and loving others. In verse 34, Jesus basically says that we are not to swear/ make an oath "a_____ a_____." That doesn't leave much room for saying nasty things, does it? In verse 44, Jesus says that loving your neighbors means also loving your e_____ and praying for those who _____ you.

MAKE YOUR CHOICE

So how am I measuring up by JESUS' standards? _____ Pretty hard, aren't they? What do I need to especially pray that Jesus will help me with today?_____

87

wednesday Matthew 6:5-15

TAKE THE CHALLENGE How much time do you actually pray each day? Are you seeing answers from God?

CHECK IT OUT The disciples really wanted to know how to have an effective prayer life. Jesus told them WHERE to pray (v. 6): _____ He told them how NOT to pray (v. 7): _____

_____ _____ He reminded them that the Heavenly Father _____ what we _____ before we even ask. Prayer is talking to God. Now let's apply the prayer he gives His disciples!

MAKE YOUR CHOICE Turn back in your Champion Quiet Time to the prayer pages. Go to a page that has a blank area and write out — word for word — the prayer Jesus gives us to use in verses 9b-13. Then pray it to Him today, and really mean the words!

Thursday Matthew 6:19-34

TAKE THE CHALLENGE Do you have a piggy bank or a bank account where you save your money to buy something you want later?

CHECK IT OUT Jesus talks about two things in this passage: Having a Heavenly Bank Account and Heavenly Focus in Life! Both of these things will keep us from worrying so much about "stuff" down here on earth. Beside each of the phrases below, put an X if you should not do this and an O if you should.

_____ Store up treasures on earth.

_____ Serve two masters: God and money.

_____ Don't worry about your life.

_____ Watch the birds and learn from them.

_____ Store up treasures in Heaven.

_____ Be devoted to only God.

_____ Worry about everything you can think of to worry about

_____ Seek first God's kingdom and His righteousness.

MAKE YOUR CHOICE Write down verse 21 here in this box: _____

_____

What do I worry about the most? _____ What does that reveal about my heart? _____

FRIDAY   Matthew 7:1-12

TAKE THE CHALLENGE

Is it okay for me to criticize someone else and find all the bad things I see in his/her life?

CHECK IT OUT

Today Jesus touches on the subject of criticism or judging others, as well as another lesson about prayer. Write out verse 1 here. "_____ _____."

Jesus is telling us that we have no right to criticize and judge others. That is His job. We have sin and wrong attitudes in our lives, also! ~ What are three ways we should be going to God with our prayer requests according to verse 7? A_____ , S_____ and K_____ What will happen if you pray this way with persistence — not giving up? _____ _____

MAKE YOUR CHOICE

Who have I criticized in the last week? _____ Do I need to ask their forgiveness? Yes / No What am I asking God for everyday without giving up? _____

SATURDAY   Matthew 7:13-29

TAKE THE CHALLENGE

If you saw a fruit tree with all rotten, black fruit hanging off it, what would you know about the inside of that tree?

CHECK IT OUT

In today's passage, Jesus is going to preach on three very picturesque issues: The Wide or Narrow Gate? Choose the narrow road that leads to _____, not the _____ road that leads to _____.
Good Fruit or Rotten Fruit? In verse 20, Jesus tells us that we recognize a true Christian by "_____ _____."
Built on the Rock or Built on the Sand? Building our life on Jesus' words is like building your house on a _____. But hearing God's Word and not applying or obeying it is like building your house on shifting _____.

MAKE YOUR CHOICE

When others watch my life as a believer, do they see the good, healthy fruit of good, godly character and kind deeds? Yes / No How am I building my life on Jesus' Word each and every day? _____ 89

Matthew 8:1–10:31

Each of the four Gospel writers presents a different picture of Jesus Christ:

WRITER	PRESENTS JESUS AS
Matthew	The King
Mark	A Servant
Luke	The Son of Man (His human side)
John	The Son of God (His godly side)

The first three Gospel writers write more from the historical narrative of Christ's actions and miracles. They do include some of Jesus' sermons. But John writes more from the focus of Jesus' claims and communications about Himself and His true identity.

Sunday Matthew 8:1-17

TAKE THE CHALLENGE

Way back over 450 years before this, the prophet Isaiah prophesied (in Isaiah 53) that the Messiah would carry away our diseases. See how He fulfilled this prophesy in today's verses.

CHECK IT OUT

Can you match the following miracle stories? (Draw lines between those which match.)

THE PERSON IN NEED

- Man with disease of leprosy
- A centurion's (policeman's) son who was paralyzed
- Demon possessed people
- The sick
- Peter's mother-in-law

THE MIRACLE PERFORMED

- Jesus said, "Go!" and the servant was healed.
- Touched her hand and the fever left
- Drove out the demon spirits with a word
- Jesus touched him and he was cured.
- Healed them

MAKE YOUR CHOICE

If Jesus lived on earth near you today, who would you ask Him to heal? _____ Why don't you pray especially for them today, and then send them a special card letting them know you are praying for their healing?

Matthew 8:18-34

TAKE THE CHALLENGE

Were you ever caught in a really bad storm? What did you do?

CHECK IT OUT

Jesus talks about the cost of following Him in verses 18-22, then He gets into a boat with His disciples. On the way across the large mountain lake, a _____ _____ came up on the sea and the _____ covered the boat. What was Jesus doing? _____ When the disciples woke Him, He rebuked them for their weak _____, and then completely calmed the _____ and the _____! That was a m_____ over nature, wasn't it? - Lastly, Jesus heals two _____ possessed by demons who were on the other side. The demon spirits went into what animals nearby? _____

MAKE YOUR CHOICE

Sometimes I may go through a difficult time in my life that seems like a storm. Who can I call on to bring His peace and calm to my life and heart? _____

Tuesday   Matthew 9:1-13

TAKE THE CHALLENGE

Do you think when Jesus forgives our sins that it is a miracle?

CHECK IT OUT

After Jesus went back to His hometown across the sea, what kind of man did some others bring to Him on a mat? _____ What did Jesus say to him? Thy (Your) _____ are forgiven! Jesus knew some of the religious leaders nearby thought He was lying when he said He could forgive sins. So what miracle did He do then to prove He had forgiven the man's sins completely? (See verses 6-7.) _____ _____ What new disciple did Jesus call to follow Him in verse 9? _____ And he's the one who later wrote the book we are reading!

MAKE YOUR CHOICE

When Jesus forgives all my sins, it is surely a miracle! It is the healing of my soul! What sins do I need to confess to Him even today? _____

wednesday Matthew 9:18-26

Has anyone important to you died in the past year? It's hard to be happy again for a long while after someone we love dies and is not here anymore.

CHECK IT OUT

A very important man — a _____ - came and bowed before Jesus. He said that his _____ had just _____. He asked Jesus to come and heal her. What did Jesus do then? _____

On His way, a bleeding woman simply _____ the edge of Jesus' _____ and she was _____. Jesus praised her strong f_____. When Jesus got to the ruler's home, a funeral was already starting. Jesus sent them away and took the girl by the _____. What did she do? _____

MAKE YOUR CHOICE

If Jesus could bring dead people back to life, He can surely answer my prayers and help me with really hard problems. What miracle would I like to see Jesus do in my life or my family? _____

Thursday Matthew 9:27-38

TAKE THE CHALLENGE

Would you be willing to pray for something important that Jesus asked you to remember in prayer?

CHECK IT OUT

X out the things below that Jesus did NOT do in these verses.

Healed two blind men   Ate at a banquet   Drove a demon out of a man who couldn't speak   Went sailing with his best friends   Went out teaching and preaching all over Galilee Healed people with every kind of disease and sickness   Tried to get at least eight hours of sleep per night   Had great compassion on the crowds of helpless people   Asked the disciples to pray for people to help reach others for Him

MAKE YOUR CHOICE

Jesus asked His disciples to pray for more people to be willing to go and reach the world's harvest of unsaved people — for Him. Am I praying daily for missionaries and preachers — and that God might send ME someday?

FRIDAY — Matthew 10:1-10

TAKE THE CHALLENGE

What do you think a disciple of Jesus needs to be able to do?

CHECK IT OUT

Can you find all 12 apostles in the WORD SEARCH? (Peter, Andrew, James (twice), John, Philip, Bartholomew, Thomas, Matthew, Thaddaeus, Simon, Judas) Now write down one traveling rule Jesus gave them: "_____

_____."

```
M N U B P I L I H P A
A O J O H N B V D E N
T M J U D A S U S T D
T I E J A M E S L E R
H S E M A J B V D R E
E S U E A D D A H T W
W E M O L O H T R A B
A S A M O H T A L R M
```

MAKE YOUR CHOICE

I am Jesus' disciple if I am willing to follow and obey Him. What is one thing I know Jesus wants me to do to stay close to Him everyday? _____

SATURDAY — Matthew 10:16-31

TAKE THE CHALLENGE

As you will see today, being a disciple of Christ was not all fun and games!

CHECK IT OUT

Find three things in today's passage that let you know that being a follower or disciple of Jesus would NOT be easy. What hardships awaited them?

(1) _____

(2) _____

(3) _____

Two times (vv. 26, 28) Jesus told the disciples not to be _____. He told them that nothing could happen to them outside the Father's will, and that He even had the _____ of their _____ numbered (v. 30)!

MAKE YOUR CHOICE

What sacrifices or tough things do I have to deal with at school or in my home when I am choosing to follow Jesus and live for Him? _____

Matthew 10:32–12:50

"Matthew" means the gift of the Lord. His gospel was written to the Jewish people to answer questions they had about Jesus. Do you know any Jewish people or have any Jewish friends? The Old Testament closed with God's people looking for their long promised King and Messiah. Matthew's gospel shows Jesus as that King. He quotes from the Old Testament more than any of the other Gospel writers. He wanted the Jews to know that Jesus fulfilled all the Old Testament prophecies about Him as Messiah.

Sunday Matthew 10:32-42

TAKE THE CHALLENGE

If you could have walked and talked with Jesus on earth, what would you have asked Him about?

CHECK IT OUT

Jesus is finishing up His final words of instruction to the twelve disciples here. Number the things He taught them in the order you find them in the passage:

_____ I came to divide people, not to bring peace.

_____ Whoever receives you receives Me.

_____ The Father recognizes those who praise Christ.

_____ Anyone who loves any others more than Me is not worthy of Me.

_____ Whoever loses his life for My sake will find it.

MAKE YOUR CHOICE

In verse 42, Jesus says if I just give a _____ of _____ _____ to a child, I will not lose my reward. That's not a very hard task, is it? Who can I give a drink of cold water to today and let them know I care and Jesus cares? (name) _____

monday

Matthew 11:1-11

TAKE THE CHALLENGE

Remember John the Baptist – the prophet dressed in animal skins? Well, he had been in prison for quite some time while Jesus' fame had been spreading.

CHECK IT OUT

John wanted to know whether all the miracles he was hearing about meant that Jesus was truly the promised Messiah. Write down at least three things Jesus told the disciples to go back and report or show him (vv. 4-6): (1) _____

(2) _____

(3) _____ What great honor did Jesus bestow on John the Baptist in verse11?_____

_____

MAKE YOUR CHOICE

John the Baptist witnessed for the Savior wherever he was. How have I been a witness for Jesus Christ lately — and where have I witnessed for Him?

_____

_____

Tuesday   Matthew 11:20-30

TAKE THE CHALLENGE

Do you ever feel really tired and stressed out? Jesus has an invitation for you!

CHECK IT OUT

Unscramble the city names below of places where Jesus did miracles, and yet they did not respond to Him and were unrepentant (unwilling to turn from their sin to Him): **ADETHASIB** _ _ _ _ _ _ _ _ _

NODIS _ _ _ _ _   **RETY** _ _ _ _

CREAPUMAN _ _ _ _ _ _ _ _ _

Finish filling out the invitation from Jesus:

Dear _____ (your name), "_____ unto me, all you who labour and are _____ _____ , and I will _____ _____ _____ " …."For my yoke is _____, and my burden is _____." Love, Jesus

MAKE YOUR CHOICE

What is weighing me down in my life or causing me to feel anxious or stressed? _____

_____ How can I accept Jesus' invitation to have His rest and peace today? _____

95

wednesday — Matthew 12:1-13

TAKE THE CHALLENGE

Have you ever been reprimanded or punished for doing something good? How did that make you feel? Well, Jesus experienced this, too.

CHECK IT OUT

Jesus and the disciples were rebuked by the P_____ for picking some _____ and eating it on the Sabbath Day. In verse 8, Jesus replies, "For the _____ of _____ is _____ even of the _____ day." Then He went into the synagogue (Jewish church) and healed a man with a shriveled _____. What did the Pharisees do after these two incidents? (Look down at verse 14 to find out.) Plotted how they could _____ _____. How sad!

MAKE YOUR CHOICE

There are people who don't like us to stand up for Jesus and help others in His name. They might even make things hard for us, as Christians. Do I know anyone like this? _____ Am I praying for them to get saved? Yes / No

Thursday — Matthew 12:22-29

TAKE THE CHALLENGE

A demon-possessed person is one who is controlled and inhabited by demon spirits. Demons are Satan's evil "angel" spirits. They always bring destruction and pain.

CHECK IT OUT

The demon-possessed man who was brought to Jesus in this story was both _____ and _____. When Jesus healed him, he could both _____ and _____. But the jealous Pharisees accused Jesus of driving out the demons by the power of _____, the _____ of the demons/devils. Jesus explained to them that you can't be AGAINST something and be FOR it at the same time. He let them know that He drove out demons by the _____ of _____ (v. 28).

MAKE YOUR CHOICE

When Satan wants to hurt or trouble me, Who can I call on to immediately drive him away? _____ What am I doing every day to get the upper hand over Satan's attacks? _____

FRIDAY — Matthew 12:30-36

TAKE THE CHALLENGE

What comes out of my heart that shows in my life – words or actions?

CHECK IT OUT

Jesus said in verse 30 that anyone who is not _____ Him is _____ Him! He's still speaking to the Pharisees here. What does He call them in verse 34? _____ of _____. He goes on to say that the _____ man brings _____ things out of his heart, but the _____ man brings up _____ things out of an evil heart. What will we all give an account of at the judgment (v. 36)? _____

MAKE YOUR CHOICE

It's pretty unnerving to know that the Heavenly Father is listening to everything I say. What kind of talk comes out of my mouth sometimes that hurts or offends God? _____ _____ Do I need to confess it as sin? _____

SATURDAY — Matthew 12:43-50

TAKE THE CHALLENGE

Does Jesus consider me to be His brother or sister? Find out today.

CHECK IT OUT

Jesus tells us the habits of evil spirits in verses 43–45 here. Then while He is talking to the crowd, His mother and brothers wait outside to speak with Him. When Jesus was told, He said that His disciples were such a part of His life now that THEY were His _____ and His _____. Write out verse 50 here: "_____ _____"

MAKE YOUR CHOICE

What do I need to do in order to be counted as one of Jesus' brothers or sisters? _____ _____ Am I ? Yes/ No What is God's will for me today? _____

chart your cours

Farmers, fishermen, BIG waves and small fish! What could all of this mean to me?

Read on and find out!

Matthew 13:1-23

TAKE THE CHALLENGE

John Deere, here I come!

CHECK IT OUT

Today's passage is a parable (a story with a spiritual message) about the four soils. Match the type of soil with the kind of hearer it represents:

By the path (wayside, road)	hears the Word, receives with joy, but no root
	hears the Word, but worries and riches choke it
On stony ground	
Among thorns	hears and understands the Word & becomes fruitful for God
Good soil	hears the Word but does not understand it

MAKE YOUR CHOICE

What kind of soil am I?_____

What do I do with God's Word when I hear it taught?_____

Am I producing fruit in my life?_____ How do I know?

_____

98

Matthew 13:24-43

TAKE THE CHALLENGE

More farmer stories?

Jesus tells three more parables in today's passage. As Christians, we have to live among those who don't know Jesus and don't make godly choices. Who does the wheat represent in the parable?_____ Whom do the tares (weeds) represent? _____

How can I live for God in this sinful world?_____
_____ What "weapons" for battle can I use?_____
_____ What should always influence my choices?_____

Tuesday Matthew 13:44-58

TAKE THE CHALLENGE

No respect at home!

In verses 53-58 Jesus comes back to His home-town of Nazareth. How do the people respond to Jesus' teaching?_____
_____

Who do they claim Jesus is in verse 55?_____ Was this true?_____
Why did they fail to recognize Jesus?_____
_____ What kept Jesus from doing many miracles in this town (v. 58)?_____

How is my faith meter? Do I have faith that God is omnipotent (all-powerful) and can do anything?_____ What situation do I need to claim God's power to help me with today?_____

99

wednesday Matthew 14:1-21

Get your head around this!

CHECK IT OUT

If you've gone to church since you were small, then you've heard parts of today's passage many times. What is something new that you read today that you never realized before?_____

How mind-boggling is it to think of 5,000+ people being fed by five loaves and two small fish?_____

How does this miracle make me feel about Jesus?_____
_____

MAKE YOUR CHOICE

The beginning of this Scripture talks about the death of Jesus' cousin and close friend, John the Baptist. Have I ever lost someone close to me? _____ How does knowing that Jesus experienced the pain of losing someone to death make me feel about His ability to understand how I feel?_____

Thursday Matthew 14:22-36

TAKE THE CHALLENGE

It's a ghost!

CHECK IT OUT

Today, Jesus sends the disciples in a boat to the other side of a huge lake. What did Jesus do while the disciples were starting across the lake?_____

What did Jesus do that scared the disciples?_____
_____ Who asked to walk to Jesus on the water?_____ Why did he begin to sink?_____
_____

MAKE YOUR CHOICE

I can trust Jesus even though the circumstances in my life might feel like high winds and crashing waves. What is one problem that I want to ask Jesus to help me with today?_____
_____ Now, I will take time to pray about this!

FRIDAY Matthew 15:1-20

Wash your hands!

CHECK IT OUT

The Pharisees were upset because the disciples were eating grain out of a field without washing their hands. They claimed that this made them "unclean". What did Jesus say truly makes a person "unclean" in verses 19-20?

_____

MAKE YOUR CHOICE

Look at the list below. Circle the things that I sometimes do that make me "unclean" before a Holy God: *watch TV shows I shouldn't   talk rudely to others   laugh at a dirty joke   read magazines or books that are not pleasing to God   listen to music with bad lyrics* What do I need to do to make myself "clean" again before God (hint: check out 1 John 1:9)?_____

SATURDAY Matthew 15:21-39

TAKE THE CHALLENGE Jesus feeds a big crowd, part 2!

Check out some numbers from today's QT passage.

CHECK IT OUT

There were 4,000 _____.

They had been there three _____.

The disciples had seven _____

and a few _____.

How much was left over?_____

MAKE YOUR CHOICE

Jesus proves again today that He is the God of the impossible situation. When things are hard in my life, Whom can I turn to and trust?_____
What situation would I like to take to Jesus in prayer right now?_____
_____ I will share this prayer request with my Mom, Dad, or Olympian leader so that they can pray for me, too!

101

christy rc rs

Life...
Death...
Protection...
Prediction...
Provision...
Forgiveness!

The Bible is jam-packed with life lessons for you and me!

Sunday   Matthew 16:1-12

TAKE THE CHALLENGE

The lesson from the lunch

CHECK IT OUT

"You forgot the bread!"..."No, YOU forgot the bread!" The disciples forgot to take bread as they crossed the lake in a boat with Jesus. What did Jesus tell them to watch out for in verse 6?
_____ What did the "leaven" (yeast) represent? _____
Why was it important for the disciples to recognize false teaching? _____

MAKE YOUR CHOICE

False teachings are dangerous. How can I know if something I hear about God or Jesus is true or false? (Circle all that apply)
~ Write to the newspaper ~ Check it out in the Bible
~ Ask my Pastor ~ Ask my parents ~ Ask my friend, Cody

monday

Matthew 16:13-23

TAKE THE CHALLENGE

Protection... at what price?

CHECK IT OUT

Peter loved Jesus. In verse 16 who does he say that Jesus is?_____ However, his love for Jesus also caused him to want to protect Jesus. In verses 21-22, what did Peter say would never happen ?_____

Why do you think Jesus rebuked Peter so harshly? _____ _____ Would we be able to be saved if Jesus hadn't died in our place on the cross?_____

MAKE YOUR CHOICE

Sometimes our love for someone causes us to want to protect them rather than watch them go through something hard. But, sometimes, the hard things are what cause us to grow closer to Jesus. What is something hard that happened to someone I love that drew them closer to Jesus?_____

Tuesday Matthew 16:24-17:13

TAKE THE CHALLENGE

A once in a lifetime experience!

CHECK IT OUT

Pretend that you are a newspaper reporter and you are breaking the big story found in today's passage. What would your headline be?_____

What three men were involved? _____ _____ _____ What happened to Jesus?_____ _____ Who else was with Him?_____

Who did the disciples say they thought had to come back before Jesus was raised from the dead?_____ Who did the disciples now understand that the "Elijah" prophecy was speaking about in verse 13? _____

MAKE YOUR CHOICE

If I have accepted Jesus as my Savior, that is my awesome, once-in-a-lifetime experience! This is how it happened:

_____

wednesday Matthew 17:14-27

TAKE THE CHALLENGE

Need cash? Go fishing!?!

Jesus and the disciples come to a new town in verse 24. What was the name of the town?

_____

What did the tax collectors want Jesus to pay?_____

Draw a picture in the TV screen above to show how Jesus provided the money for Peter to pay the tax. It would be a big news story if this happened today!

MAKE YOUR CHOICE

One of God's names is "Jehovah-Jireh" which means the Lord will provide. How have I seen God provide for me or my family? (example: providing a good church, godly friends, etc.) _____

Thursday Matthew 18:1-20

TAKE THE CHALLENGE

How do we handle SIN?

What do you do if another Christian sins against you? Jesus tells us how to handle this situation in verses 15-17. Write the steps to follow here: Step 1 — verse 15: Go to him _____, and discuss the problem. If he will not listen... Step 2 -- verse 16: Take _____ with you. If he still will not listen... Step 3 — verse 17a: Take it before the _____. If he still will not listen... Step 4 — verse 17b: Treat him as a _____ or a _____. Does this mean that we treat someone rudely and horribly? No! The purpose of putting an unrepentant person out of the church is to make him WANT to repent so he can be welcomed back into the church.

MAKE YOUR CHOICE

My responsibility before God is to be concerned with my own spiritual life. Is there someone I need to forgive today? **Yes / No** Who? _____ _Why?_____ But, is there someone I need to ask to forgive me? **Yes / No** Who? _____

FRIDAY — Matthew 18:21-35

Forgiveness, the sequel.

Jesus tells the story today of a man who was forgiven much, but he, himself, could not forgive even a small amount. Put the events from today's passage in order.

___Man chokes fellow servant

___Man is thrown in jail

___Man appears before the king

___Man pleads for mercy from the king

___Man leaves the palace

___Man demands his few dollars from fellow servant

___The king orders man's wife & children be sold to pay his debt

___Man has fellow servant thrown into prison

___Man finds servant who owes him money

How many times does Jesus say that I should forgive someone who wrongs me (v. 22)?_____ How much of my sin did Jesus forgive when He saved me?_____ Do I have any right to withhold forgiveness from someone who asks me?_____

SATURDAY — Matthew 19:1-15

Jesus Loves Kids!

Do you ever feel like the adults in your life don't take you seriously? Jesus reminds the disciples just how important children are to Him. Write verse 14 here: _____

_____

_____

_____

Jesus Loves _____
(Write your name here). Now, I will pray: *Thank you so much, Jesus, for loving me like You do. Help me show You how much I love You, by living in ways that please and honor You today. Amen.*

Chart your course

Have you ever done some yard work or babysitting for someone? How much did you get paid? If you worked for a day in Jesus' time you would get paid a denarius, which was a day's pay! A denarius would be about sixteen cents in today's economy. Not much, huh?

Sunday — Matthew 19:16-30

TAKE THE CHALLENGE

Can a camel fit through a needle?

CHECK IT OUT

What did the rich young ruler want to know (v. 16)? _____

What did Jesus tell him that he had to do?

_____

_____

Is it really possible for someone to keep all those commandments all the time without sinning? **Yes / No** Why? _____

At the end of verse, 21 Jesus tells the man two little words that he must do to gain eternal life. What are they? F_ _ _ _ _ _ M _.

MAKE YOUR CHOICE

Am I following Jesus by how I live my life? (Circle things you have done.) Have I: Given my life to Jesus? Asked forgiveness for my sins? Given some of my money to God? Been kind to others?

monday

Matthew 20:1-16

TAKE THE

How fair is THAT? How come they get the same money for less work?

CHECK IT OUT

In today's passage, a _____ hires some workers for the day. He agrees to pay them a _____ (Look it up at "Chart Your Course" to see how much that was worth!) for a day's work. He then hires more workers throughout the day - some just before quitting time - yet everyone receives the same pay. Color the spaces with dots to find out what this is called.

MAKE YOUR CHOICE

In the same way as our story, Jesus offers salvation to all people whether they are a small child, with their whole life to live for Him, or an older person who is dying. How has God shown me His grace in my life?

_____

Tuesday

Matthew 20:29-34

TAKE THE CHALLENGE

What do you want me to do for you?

CHECK IT OUT

Close your eyes for a moment and picture yourself sitting on a sidewalk, unable to see. Feel the hard ground under your seat. Smell the dust as people walk by. Hear them talking or laughing. . . . But you cannot see them because you are blind. - If this was you, what would you want more than anything? _____ What would you feel for the One who made this dream come true in your life? _____ _____ What does the Bible say the two blind men did when Jesus restored their sight (v.34)?_____

MAKE YOUR CHOICE

If Jesus asked me what He could do for me today, what would I say? _____ I will tell Him about this right now in prayer, and write it in my prayer pages.

wednesday Matthew 21:1-17

 TAKE THE CHALLENGE

Have you ever ridden a donkey?

 CHECK IT OUT

What is the word that the people used to praise Jesus? H _ _ _ _ _ _

How did Jesus get into the city? _____

What does verse 4 tell you about why Jesus came into Jerusalem that way?_____

Why was Jesus angry when He came into the temple area?_____

 MAKE YOUR CHOICE

I have much to praise Jesus for in my life. Sing a song of praise to Jesus right now. — I can't HEAR you!

Thursday Matthew 21:23-27

TAKE THE CHALLENGE

Who are you and how do you do these things?

 CHECK IT OUT

The Pharisees wanted to try to trap Jesus by their words, but Jesus turned their trap on them! Jesus asked them about John the Baptist's ministry... was it from _____ or of _____? What did they finally answer in verse 27? We _____.

Did they really know? **Yes / No** Why wouldn't they answer Jesus truthfully? _____

MAKE YOUR CHOICE

Am I ever tempted to say, "I don't know" to avoid getting in trouble for something? Circle every other letter to find out what this is really called. X L Z Y A I S N W G

FRIDAY — Matthew 22:1-14

See you at the ball!

CHECK IT OUT

Imagine that you have been invited to a "red carpet" event. It is a gala evening with amazing food, guests, and even brand new clothes to wear! Would you go? In this story, Jesus illustrates how He invites everyone to Heaven, but some people will refuse to come. Why do you think someone would reject Jesus' offer of salvation? _____

How many people does Jesus want to be saved? _____

MAKE YOUR CHOICE

If I know Jesus as my Savior, Jesus wants me to invite others to know Him, too! What is one way that I could witness to someone I know? _____

SATURDAY — Matthew 22:15-22

It's a trap!

CHECK IT OUT

Again, the Pharisees try to trap Jesus with a hard question about paying taxes. Jesus foils their plan by answering in a way that only God the Son could. Verse 22 tells how the Pharisees felt about Jesus' teaching when He was done. They _____.

Did this cause them to give their hearts to God? _____

_____

MAKE YOUR CHOICE

Jesus does things every day to amaze me. Look out your window. List five things that you can see out your window that God created. _____

_____ _____ _____

_____ Now thank God for His amazing love, power, and imagination.

ch rt y rc rs

The Rapture is when Jesus comes back to take all Christians to Heaven with Him. How can I be ready for His return? Check out this week to find out!

Sunday Matthew 22:34-46

TAKE THE CHALLENGE

Is it all about me?

CHECK IT OUT

A Pharisee asked Jesus what the "greatest" commandment was. Write what Jesus said were the first and second greatest commandments on the lines below: #1 – Love ____ Lord ____ G___ with all ____ h_____ and with all ____ s_____ and with all ____ m_____. #2 – Love ____ n_____ as _____. Who are you supposed to love MORE than you love yourself, according to these verses? _____ and my _____.

MAKE YOUR CHOICE

How much do I love God and others? Do I show it by how I act? Do I put others first and make my time with God a priority? God, help me to show that I love You by_____.

Matthew 23:1-12

TAKE THE CHALLENGE The twilight zone of honor!

CHECK IT OUT

Jesus' teachings are so opposite to what the world says that often they may seem crazy to those who don't know Him. In this "get ahead ...its all about me" world, Jesus says humility and a servant's heart are what's important to Him. Look for these other words for humility in the word search below: lowly, meek, modest. Now look for these words that mean the opposite of humility: pride, brag, bold

L	T	U	B	L	E	S	S	I	N	G
O	T	S	E	D	O	M	V	Y	P	A
W	T	S	D	R	A	E	D	D	E	B
L	J	E	I	U	K	E	O	L	R	W
Y	T	N	R	P	O	K	V	O	K	A
S	Y	F	P	K	G	A	R	B	N	H
I	S	A	A	C	O	B	V	D	W	A
A	R	E	T	H	G	U	A	L	R	M

MAKE YOUR CHOICE

How am I doing at being humble? Do I (circle the ones that apply): brag, talk a lot, do things for attention, have to be right, boss others, make rules, talk negatively about others? How do I need to change?

Tuesday Matthew 23:13-26

TAKE THE CHALLENGE

How often do you wash the dishes at your house?

CHECK IT OUT

Jesus challenged the Pharisees about keeping the inside of their dishes as clean as the outside. Was He really talking about dishes? No! He was talking about their hearts and how they followed the rules but refused to change in their hearts. Think about some ways someone might follow God so that people could see it. What are some ways people might sin secretly so that no one except God would know? _____

_____

MAKE YOUR CHOICE

How are my dishes? Are they clean on the outside AND on the inside? Yes / No If I know Jesus, but I mess up and sin, I can talk to Him in prayer, confess my sin and ask His forgiveness. What do I need to confess and ask forgiveness for right now?

_____ Take time right now to talk to Jesus.

wednesday Matthew 23:27-39

Been to the cemetery lately?

Have you ever been to a cemetery and seen flowers and gifts left on the graves? People do this to honor and remember their loved ones who have died. The Pharisees were doing things like this to make their lives "look" beautiful on the outside, but yet they wouldn't deal with sin in their own hearts. Write what Jesus says to them in verse 27 here:_"_____

_____

_____ "

How is my heart? (Circle one.) Not too pretty / Sinful / White & clean / Hateful / Loving What would Jesus say to me about my heart if He saw it (which He does) right now?_____

Thursday Matthew 24:1-14

TAKE THE CHALLENGE   What's the price?

Verse 9 talks about the persecution of Christians. You may not be facing persecution for your faith right now, but many Christians around the world are. What would it be like to live in a country where you or your parents would go to jail if you were caught reading your Bible, witnessing, or going to church? _____

What would you have to do differently than you do right now?

_____

Do you think you would read your Bible more than you do now? _____ Why? _____

I will take time right now to pray for those who are suffering for their faith in foreign countries. I'll also take time to praise Jesus that I can read my Bible, pray, and go to church whenever I want to without fear.

FRIDAY — Matthew 24:15-31

TAKE THE CHALLENGE

Is it Him?

CHECK IT OUT

Jesus is telling His disciples how they will know that it is really Him when He returns for His children. Write the signs He gives them out of the following verses: Verse 27 - His coming will be like _____ that comes from the east and can be seen in the west. Verse 30 - He will come in the clouds with p_____ and g_____. Verse 31 - He will send His a_____ and there will be a loud t_____ call.

MAKE YOUR CHOICE

Am I ready for the Rapture? (See "Chart Your Course") Is there a person that I want to be saved so that they can one day go to Heaven? Write his name here _____. I will write them a letter this week telling them what Jesus has done for me!

SATURDAY — Matthew 24:32-51

TAKE THE CHALLENGE

When will Jesus come?

CHECK IT OUT

Who is the only One who knows the exact time when Jesus will return? (See verse 36.) _____

Verse 42 tells us how we should act until Jesus returns.

Write it here: _____

_____

What does it mean to keep watch or be watchful? _____

_____

MAKE YOUR CHOICE

How can I be like the wise servant in verses 45-46? _____
_____ What are some things that I would like to be "caught doing" at the exact moment when Jesus returns? _____
_____

25 WEEKLY PASSAGES COVERED
Matthew 25:1-26:56

Just before His arrest and trial, Jesus used everyday objects to teach His disciples important principles. As you study this week, circle the objects that you find in chapter 25

sheep goats talents
oil lamps master
servants

Sunday   Matthew 25:1-13

TAKE THE CHALLENGE

When you are invited to be part of a wedding party, you want to be READY when the bride and groom arrive, right?

CHECK IT OUT

Because they had to wait a long time, what did all the virgins do while they were waiting?

_____

What did the foolish virgins forget to take with them? _____ for their _____ Were they READY when the bridegroom arrived? _____

MAKE YOUR CHOICE

To be READY for a test at school, I need to _____.
To be READY to go to church on time, I need to _____.
To be READY for a big game, I need to _____.
To be READY when Jesus comes back, I need to _____.

monday — Matthew 25:14-30

TAKE THE CHALLENGE

If your Mom and Dad leave you at home with chores while they are gone, do you want to prove that you are responsible when they come back?

CHECK IT OUT

How many talents did the servant with five talents gain?_____ How many talents did the servant with two talents gain? _____

What excuse did the lazy servant give for hiding his talent? "I was _____."

MAKE YOUR CHOICE

When I am blessed with money, responsibilities, or opportunities, I (Check all that apply to you!) . . _____ Am lazy and wait for someone to make me work _____ Quickly do what I can to do the job right _____ Do nothing and hope no one notices _____ Do nothing because I am afraid of making a mistake

Tuesday — Matthew 25:31-46

TAKE THE CHALLENGE

Did you know that how we care for others shows what we think of Christ?

CHECK IT OUT

Who was on the right hand of Christ? _____
How did they treat the hungry?_____
The stranger?_____
The sick?_____
Who was on the left hand of Christ?_____
How did they treat the hungry?_____
The stranger?_____
The sick?_____

MAKE YOUR CHOICE

TODAY, here's what I can do to show kindness to (write a name of someone who needs help) _____ (and to Christ!) _____
_____(Check here when you DO IT!) ▢

115

wednesday
Matthew 26:1-16

What is Jesus worth to you?

CHECK IT OUT

To show how much she valued her Savior, what kind of ointment (perfume) did this woman pour on Him? _____ (This cost about 300 days' wages!) In contrast, Judas was willing to SELL Jesus to the authorities for how much money? _____ (This was the price of a common slave, about 120 days' wages.)

MAKE YOUR CHOICE

I give _____ of my money to God. I spend _____ minutes every day getting to know God (reading my Bible) and talking to God (praying). Your answers to these questions tell how much Jesus is really worth to you!

Thursday
Matthew 26:17-29

TAKE THE CHALLENGE

Think of some symbols that help you remember important things.

CHECK IT OUT

Jesus introduced His disciples to two symbols that we still use today to remind us to think about His sacrifice for our sins. What reminds us of His body?_____
What reminds us of His blood?_____
Why is His blood so precious (v. 28)? It was shed for the _____ of _____.

MAKE YOUR CHOICE

The next time my church family celebrates Communion, I will focus on Jesus' _____ and His _____.

FRIDAY — Matthew 26:30-46

TAKE THE CHALLENGE

This may have been the hardest time for Jesus in His life here on earth.

CHECK IT OUT

How did Jesus feel as He faced the fact that He would be crucified?_____

_____ What did He ask His disciples to do for Him?_____

What did He find them doing?_____

_____

MAKE YOUR CHOICE

Before I think badly of the disciples for falling asleep:
When was the last time I got sleepy in church?_____
How often do I sleep in instead of getting up to do my Quiet Time?_____

SATURDAY — Matthew 26:47-56

TAKE THE CHALLENGE

All used different objects or actions, but all were used of God.

CHECK IT OUT

What sign did Judas use?_____

What weapons did the crowd use?_____

What weapon did Jesus' companion use?_____

Jesus said this all happened to fulfill the _____ (v. 56).

MAKE YOUR CHOICE

When bad things happen, I will remember that God will always carry out His plans.
Pray today: *Dear Jesus, when bad or sad things happen in my life that hurt me, help me to become a better person and not a bitter person. I want to grow to be more like You in both the hard things as well as the happy things I experience. Thank You for always being here with me through every circumstance. I love You. Amen*

During Christ's last days on earth, many people treated Him badly. Match those individuals with their reactions after realizing how they had hurt Jesus:

PETER
JUDAS
PILATE
CENTURION

- Washed his hands
- Said, "Truly this was the Son of God
- Hanged himself
- Wept bitterly

Sunday — Matthew 26:57-75

TAKE THE CHALLENGE

Have you ever been falsely accused? What would Jesus do?

CHECK IT OUT

What kind of evidence were they looking for (v.59)? _____ What was Jesus' response v. 63)?_____

When asked a direct question, Jesus: (check the right one)

_____ **Tried to defend himself.,**

_____ **Only spoke the truth.**

MAKE YOUR CHOICE

Lord, help me to respond to evil people as You did. When I am attacked or falsely accused, I will _____
_____

Matthew 27:1-14

TAKE THE CHALLENGE

What happens when someone won't seek or accept God's forgiveness?

CHECK IT OUT

What did Judas say to admit he was wrong?

_____ _____ _____

Just because he felt guilty, did that change the consequences of his sin?_____

What did Judas do instead of dealing with the consequences of his sin?_____

_____

MAKE YOUR CHOICE

Lord, help me understand that You died to take the punishment for my sin and though I must face the consequences, I don't have to punish myself.

Tuesday   Matthew 27:15-32

TAKE THE CHALLENGE

Trading places with a criminal?

CHECK IT OUT

What was the name of the criminal who was released instead of Jesus?_____

Pilate asked the crowd what crime Jesus had committed. Did they answer?_____

Did Jesus protest this injustice?_____

MAKE YOUR CHOICE

Help me to realize that Jesus willingly traded places with _____ to take the punishment for my sin.

wednesday — Matthew 27:33-50

Read about the darkest day of Jesus' life!

CHECK IT OUT

How many hours of darkness were there?_____

Jesus took upon Himself the sin of the world, and

God is too holy to look upon sin. What was Jesus'

agonizing cry in verse 46 "_____ _____

_____ _____ _____ _____

_____ _____ _____?"

MAKE YOUR CHOICE

There could be no greater way for God to prove His

_____ for me!

Thursday — Matthew 27:51-66

When Jesus died, the whole world responded!

CHECK IT OUT

What happened to the earth?_____

What happened to the tombs?_____

What happened to the temple curtain?_____

(This curtain symbolized the separation between a holy

God and sinful man. By Jesus' death, that separation is

now abolished!)

MAKE YOUR CHOICE

I praise God that my sin doesn't have to _____

me from God!

FRIDAY — Matthew 28:1-10

This is the best part of the story!

CHECK IT OUT

Our Savior is not dead, He is _____!

On what day of the week did they find the tomb

empty?_____

MAKE YOUR CHOICE

Every Sunday, as I go to church, I will celebrate with great _____ that Jesus is alive! What would my life have been like if Jesus had stayed dead forever?

_____

SATURDAY — Matthew 28:11-20

Pay attention! Here are Jesus' last words on earth!

Jesus said:

GO (to whom?)_____

TEACH (what?)_____

BAPTIZE (how?) _____

That's a big job! How can we do it? In the power of

_____ because He is _____ with us!

MAKE YOUR CHOICE

I will obey Jesus' last words by sharing the Gospel with _____ this week. Have I obeyed Jesus command to be baptized? Yes / No This is the first way I show others that I have been raised up to "new life" in Jesus Christ after I become a Christian.

27

James 1:1-3:10

Let's look at the author of this amazing little book . . .

The name of James means Supplanter!
(Supplanter means one who overthrows someone else and takes their position or place.)

~ **Probably the half-brother of Jesus Christ!**

~ **Didn't believe in Jesus until after the resurrection!**

~ **A leader in the Jerusalem church.**

~ **Nicknamed "Camel Knees" because he knelt to pray so much!**

Sunday   James 1:1-8

TAKE THE CHALLENGE   Did anyone ever say, "Bless you!" after you sneezed? What does it mean to be "blessed"?

CHECK IT OUT   Match the following (draw lines between) from the verses:

When you encounter trials/temptations	* 12 tribes
Servant of God and Jesus	* Ask of God
If you lack wisdom	* Like a wave of the sea or surf
Scattered abroad among the nations	* Unstable in all his ways
He who doubts or wavers	* Consider it all joy
Double-minded man	* James

MAKE YOUR CHOICE   What are some things I could learn through tests, trials, or tough things that come into my life? _____

_____

James 1:9-18

TAKE THE CHALLENGE

Do you ever wonder what our crowns in Heaven will look like?

CHECK IT OUT

James uses lots of word pictures in his little book. Put the proper verse numbers under the picture they illustrate: Choose from verses 11, 12 and 17.

_____   _____   _____

Number the following four words in order of their conceptions or births (vv. 14-15): _____ sin _____ death _____ lust _____ temptation

MAKE YOUR CHOICE

How can I have victory over temptation that comes my way today?

_____

Tuesday   James 1:19-27

TAKE THE CHALLENGE

Do you know people who talk the talk (talk about God) but don't walk the walk (live godly lives)?

CHECK IT OUT

Verse 19 gives some very good advice:

(1) We should be _____ to _____.

(2) We should be _____ to _____.

(3) We should be _____ to _____.

Interesting that God gave us two ears (to listen) and only one _____ (to speak)! Which of these pictures is like the Bible, God's Word, as we look into it? (Circle one.)

MAKE YOUR CHOICE

How am I doing at listening more than talking? _____ What did God's Word show me about myself today, and how will I work on it? _____

wednesday — James 2:1-9

TAKE THE CHALLENGE

How do you treat foreign, poor, or underprivileged people?

CHECK IT OUT

This whole passage basically tells us what people (Christians) act like who don't live or practice God's Royal Law: "Thou shalt (you shall) _____ thy (your) _____ as _____." How did the people in verses 1 to 7 not do this? _____

_____

_____

MAKE YOUR CHOICE

Write down an area in which you've failed in or displeased God in the last few weeks. _____

_____ Have you confessed your sin to God? YES / NO

Thursday — James 2:10-18

TAKE THE CHALLENGE

Did anyone ever say, "Bless you!" after you sneezed? What does it mean to be "blessed"?

CHECK IT OUT

If you drop even one drop of ink in a glass of water, it makes the water dark and cloudy, doesn't it? Look closely at verse 10. It tells us that someone can keep the _____ _____ and just mess up at _____ _____, and they are _____ of breaking _____ of it. So even if you do really well at obeying one thing and yet mess up in another, you are still (circle one) a sincere person / a sinner.

MAKE YOUR CHOICE

Write down an area in which you've failed or displeased God in the last few weeks. _____

Have you confessed your sin to God? YES / NO

124

FRIDAY

James 2:19-26

TAKE THE CHALLENGE

Did you ever think about the fact that the devil himself actually believes there is one God?

CHECK IT OUT

Count how many times you see the word faith in these verses. Write the number in this box:

This passage is a reminder that if we truly have faith in God, it will show by how we treat others, and by the good things (deeds or works) we choose to do. Name two Old Testament folks who proved their faith in God by their good deeds: _____ _____ and _____

MAKE YOUR CHOICE

Ephesians 2:8-9 reminds us we are saved only by faith, not works — but this passage in James reminds me that my faith needs to _____ by the good things I do as a Christian.

SATURDAY

James 3:1-10

TAKE THE CHALLENGE

Has your mouth gotten you into trouble lately?

CHECK IT OUT

James, in his colorful writing style, uses lots of word pictures in this passage to describe how important our tongue is. It can either delight others or destroy others. The choice is up to us. Circle the word pictures he uses in the list below, then draw one of them in the box provided.

bits in horses' mouths / bicycle wheels / bowling balls / ship's rudder / a fire spark

a match / tree limbs / wild animals / a poisonous snake

MAKE YOUR CHOICE

Write out verse 10 _____

Have I ever talked back to my Mom right after saying good, kind things to a friend on the phone? YES/ NO

125

James 3:11-5:20

Why did Jesus' half-brother write this letter?

- To encourage persecuted Jewish Christians scattered across many countries
- He was the leader in the Jerusalem church.
- To instruct hurting believers in how to face their difficulties and live the Christian life
- Because he was in Jerusalem and they were far away

Sunday James 3:11-18

TAKE THE CHALLENGE

How has your tongue gotten you in trouble this past week?

CHECK IT OUT

These verses are about our words and God's wisdom. Match the contrasts below that James uses to describe the tongue:

sweet, fresh water   blessing
cursing   bitter salt water
olives   a grapevine

Now look at the characteristics below and write before each whether it describes earthly, devilish "wisdom" (EDW) or heavenly, godly wisdom (HGW). We did the first one for you:

HGW pure _____ selfish _____ peaceful _____ envious
_____ full of mercy _____ impartial or fair _____ boastful
_____ good fruits _____ considerate

MAKE YOUR CHOICE

Put a check ✓ by any of the characteristics of earthly wisdom you've seen in yourself. Now put an X by one godly character trait you need to work on.

monday — James 4:1-5

TAKE THE CHALLENGE

What makes adults and kids fight and quarrel so much? Why are there wars?

CHECK IT OUT

In today's chapter, James asks the same question as the one above. Write one sentence giving his answer to this question: _____

_____

_____

_____

_____

MAKE YOUR CHOICE

I cannot be a _____ of the world and a _____ _____ of God at the same time. I choose to be a _____ of God! (Do you really? YES/ NO)

Tuesday — James 4:6-10

TAKE THE CHALLENGE

Have you ever wondered how a Christian can fight the devil and be victorious over

CHECK IT OUT

James gives us a prescription for being a victorious believer in these wonderful verses. Number his seven-part instructions in the order in which he gives them (in the prescription order below).

_____ Mourn over your sin   _____ Humble yourself before God

_____ Submit to God   _____ Wash and purify your heart

_____ Come near/nigh to God _____ Resist the devil

_____ Change (your laughter to mourning)

MAKE YOUR CHOICE

Put X's next to the ones above where you are weak. Then pray and ask God to help you get victory as a Christian.

wednesday   James 4:11-17

TAKE THE CHALLENGE

Has God ever changed the plans you had for your day or your life?

CHECK IT OUT

Verses 13-16 remind us that our plans for

t_____ or t_____ could

change, since we really don't know the future. James

compares our life to a _____ that

_____ for a _____ while and then

evaporates (vanishes) away. Knowing this, we always need

to say, "If the _____ wills it, I will do this or that."

MAKE YOUR CHOICE

What is something I plan to do today or this week?

_____

Now stop and ask the LORD what His will or plan for me is.

Thursday   James 5:1-6

TAKE THE CHALLENGE

Have you ever seen a boss or employer treat his employees or workers unfairly? Did you ever do work for someone who forgot to pay you?

CHECK IT OUT

What kind of people are these verses speaking to?

_____

_____Even though verse 6

tells us these unkind men have _____ and

_____ innocent or just people, the last part of verse 4 gives

hope when it reminds us that the _____ of the workers

have been heard by the _____.

MAKE YOUR CHOICE

How do I know God hears me when I cry out to Him or am treated unfairly? _____

_____

James 5:7-12

TAKE THE CHALLENGE

Fill in the blank: When I'm _____ _____, I get very impatient!

CHECK IT OUT

Try doing the crossword puzzle below using today's passage:

ACROSS: 1- The _____ are an example of patience in suffering (v. 10). 2- The _____ (God) is standing at the door (v. 9). 3- Be _____ (vv. 7-8). 4- _____ was a godly man of patience (v. 11).

DOWN: 5- The O.T. prophets were an _____ of patience (v. 10). 6- "Be patient, therefore, brethren, unto [until] the _____ of the Lord." (v. 7)

MAKE YOUR CHOICE

I will work on being more _____ this week. _____ could come back any day and I want to be ready for Him. With whom do I have the hardest time being patient? _____

James 5:13-20

TAKE THE CHALLENGE

Can you think of two people who pray for you? How does that make you feel?

CHECK IT OUT

Match the following by drawing lines between the circles and squares:

Prayed about rain

Confess your sins to each other and pray.

HE SHOULD PRAY!

Any of you in trouble, afflicted, suffering?

He should sing psalms of praise!

So you can be healed

ELIJAH

Anyone sick?

Call the elders of the church to pray.

Anyone cheerful, happy or merry?

MAKE YOUR CHOICE

Verse 20 reminds me that anyone who turns/converts a _____ from his sinful way will help save his soul from _____. Who can I pray for right now — that God will give me courage to witness to them about Jesus' love and forgiveness? _____

129

WEEKLY PASSAGES COVERED
Proverbs 6:1-8:11

Proverbs are principles to apply to daily life! Look at these short proverbs below. They are short versions of some of those we will look at this week. (Remember that King Solomon collected all these.)

➡ A careless promise leads to being trapped.
➡ Laziness leads to poverty.
➡ God hates anything that hurts His people.
➡ Parents are God's gift to us.
➡ God values marriage very highly.
➡ God values wisdom very highly.

Sunday   Proverbs 6:1-11

TAKE THE CHALLENGE

Did you ever make a promise that you couldn't keep? Are you ever lazy?

CHECK IT OUT

Fill in the blanks with words from today's passage that mean the following:

-- Make a promise:_____

-- Lazy person:_____

-- Boss:_____

-- State of being poor:_____

MAKE YOUR CHOICE

When I am tempted to sleep late or be lazy, remind me that laziness is directly connected to being _____.

monday

Proverbs 6:12-19

TAKE THE CHALLENGE
Did you know that God is concerned about every part of you?

CHECK IT OUT
Fill in the part of your body that can be involved in these things that God hates (the last one is done for you):

Pride (also known as haughtiness) --_____

Lying--_____

Hurting others--_____

Planning wickedness--_____

Running to trouble--_____

Stirring up fights—my whole self

MAKE YOUR CHOICE
I don't want any part of me to do something to make God _____.

Which one of the above have I had trouble with? (Circle it.)

Tuesday Proverbs 6:20-35

TAKE THE CHALLENGE
Do you feel like your parents are always "on your back" about something?

CHECK IT OUT
Guess what? That's their job!

In verse 23 God says your parents' rules and teaching are like three words that start with **"L"**

L _ _ _ and **L** _ _ _ _ (both of these help you see where you're going)

L _ _ _ (and this is what its ALL about!)

MAKE YOUR CHOICE
God, thank you for my _____. Help me to _____ what they say to me.

wednesday — Proverbs 7:1-9

TAKE THE CHALLENGE

What should we do with God's words?

CHECK IT OUT

ACROSS

3. Where are we to bind God's Words?
5. My law is the _____ of your eye

DOWN

1. What you will do if you keep God's commandments
2. On what tablet are we to write God's Words?
4. Say to wisdom "you are my _____"

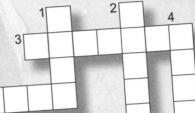

MAKE YOUR CHOICE

A proverb I will memorize this week is _____
_____.

Thursday — Proverbs 7:10-18

TAKE THE CHALLENGE

What is a woman's most important job?

CHECK IT OUT

This passage describes an **EVIL** woman.
Write down the number of the verse that says:

She never stays at home. [ ]

She is loud and stubborn. [ ]

She dresses to entice men. [ ]

She distracts men and leads them astray. [ ]

MAKE YOUR CHOICE

(Girls) I will be very careful how I _____
to please God

(Guys) I will stay away from girls who_____,
o I will stay focused on pleasing God.

FRIDAY
Proverbs 7:19-27

TAKE THE CHALLENGE

Guys, do you want to be a victim of an evil woman?

CHECK IT OUT

Fill in the number of the verse that says:

She entices men and leads them astray. ☐

She goes behind her husband's back. ☐

She flatters men with her words. ☐

The woman in these verses is beautiful and flattering, but where does she lead the men? _____

MAKE YOUR CHOICE

(Girls) I need to guard against hurting guys by how I: **Dress - Talk - Flirt** (circle any that apply)

(Guys) I need to guard my eyes from: **Magazines - TV shows - Immodest girls in my school - Sexual computer images** (circle any that apply)

SATURDAY
Proverbs 8:1-11

TAKE THE CHALLENGE

Why is LEARNING so important?

CHECK IT OUT

Write down every word in this passage that refers to learning or being wise (Hint: there are at least eight.)

_____ _____

_____ _____

_____ _____

_____ _____

_____ _____

Do you think that WISDOM is important to God? Yes / No

MAKE YOUR CHOICE

Some things that I can do to become a wiser person are_____

_____

c h r t y r c r s

Riches. Honor. Wealth. Happiness. Long Life.

GREAT! How can we get these things? Surprisingly, it has very little to do with how good a job you have or how much money you save or how many important people you know. Then what's the secret?

It's all about Wisdom.

Sunday   Proverbs 8:12-21

TAKE THE CHALLENGE   ## Is "hate" a dirty word?

CHECK IT OUT

To "fear the Lord" means to have reverence or respect for Him so much that we are afraid not to obey Him. From this passage, list four things that we are to hate if we fear the Lord

1. _____

2. _____

3. _____

4. _____

MAKE YOUR CHOICE

Lord, I need your help getting rid of _____ in my life. I know that I should hate it like You do.

monday

Proverbs 8:22-36

TAKE THE CHALLENGE
Is this passage about a PERSON or a characteristic of a person?

CHECK IT OUT
Look back at verse 12 to see who is talking in this whole chapter._____

Is this a person?_____

It could be! Look at verses 23 and 30. Who is the only PERSON who has been here forever?

_____

SO... _____ (v. 12)

equals _____ (v. 30) (see 1 Cor. 1:30)

MAKE YOUR CHOICE
If I want to have real wisdom, I really have to get close to

_____.

Tuesday

Proverbs 9:1-9

TAKE THE CHALLENGE
Do you get angry when someone corrects or instructs you?

CHECK IT OUT
If so, what does this passage call you? _____

_____

On the flip side, how does a wise man react to the

one who rebukes him? Verse 8 - He _____ him.

Verse 9 - He becomes _____.

MAKE YOUR CHOICE
God, I want to learn! Help me to learn from people who love

me enough to _____ me.

Wednesday Proverbs 9:10-18

TAKE THE CHALLENGE

Do you want to be wise?

CHECK IT OUT

"The _____ _____

_____ _____

is the beginning of wisdom," Look

back to Sunday's QT to see what this phrase means and

write it here: _____

_____

MAKE YOUR CHOICE

I want to be wise, so I know the first step is to have the

proper attitude toward _____.

Thursday Proverbs 10:1-10

TAKE THE CHALLENGE

Are you a "go-getter" or are you always waiting for someone else to do the work?

CHECK IT OUT

Two verses in this passage talk about the sin of laziness.

Can you pick them out? Verse [____] and verse [____]

In verse 4, is it likely that the lazy man will be poor

or rich? _____ What word in verse 4 means the

OPPOSITE of lazy?_____

MAKE YOUR CHOICE

I need to work on being less lazy in the area of: (Check all that apply.)

_____My school work _____Keeping my room clean

_____Helping mom around the house _____My scripture memory

FRIDAY

Proverbs 10:11-21

TAKE THE CHALLENGE

Is your tongue a tool for good or bad?

CHECK IT OUT

From this passage, list in the correct column:

Good things about the tongue	Bad things about the tongue
_____	_____
_____	_____
_____	_____
_____	_____
_____	_____

MAKE YOUR CHOICE

What I want to do with my mouth today is: (Check all that apply)

____Lie ____Criticize ____Talk a lot ____Encourage

____Listen more than I speak ____Praise God

SATURDAY

Proverbs 10:22-32

TAKE THE CHALLENGE

What do you enjoy looking forward to?

CHECK IT OUT

This passage tells what the wicked have to look forward to:

AND what the righteous have to look forward to:

Verse 24_____

Verse 24_____

Verse 25_____

Verse 25_____

Verse 27_____

Verse 27_____

Verse 28_____

Verse 28_____

MAKE YOUR CHOICE

I want my future to be _____ so I will ask God to help me be _____ today!

chrty rc rsb

David is described as "the sweet psalmist of Israel" and "a man after God's own heart." He was also a mighty warrior. Yet, he was a person (a sinner) just like you and me. We can learn much from David's life!

Sunday 1 Chronicles 10:13-11:9

TAKE THE CHALLENGE

What kind of person does great things for God?

CHECK IT OUT

Match the person with his description.

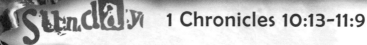

-David   - Died because he was
              unfaithful to God

-Saul   - Told the people David
              would be king

-Samuel   - Became "commander in chief"

-Joab   - Became King at Hebron

MAKE YOUR CHOICE

I want to be faithful, like _____,
_____, and _____,
so God can use me to accomplish His plan!

138

monday

1 Chronicles 11:10-19

TAKE THE CHALLENGE

Can anyone become great all on his own, with no help?

CHECK IT OUT

What kind of men supported David?_____

_____ How many men risked their

lives to bring David water?_____

What did David do with the water?_____

_____

MAKE YOUR CHOICE

In my life, I thank God for the following people who support me every day:_____
Who can I support and help so they can become all that God wants them to be?_____

Tuesday

1 Chronicles 15:1-3; 25-29

TAKE THE CHALLENGE

What should worship be like?

CHECK IT OUT

The ark of the covenant represented God's presence with the Israelites. Write the verse number that shows each of these things that were a part of how the Israelites celebrated God's presence

| | A prepared place | | Special clothing |

| | Prepared people | | Special music |

| | Rejoicing and celebrating |

MAKE YOUR CHOICE

When I worship God, I need to take more care about:
☐ How I dress ☐ How I sing ☐ How enthusiastic I am
☐ Treating the church building well

wednesday — 1 Chronicles 16:1-11

TAKE THE CHALLENGE

How important is it that we remember to praise God?

CHECK IT OUT

David set aside a whole group of people whose only job was to praise God! Who was the head of the group?_____ What instruments did they use?_____

David wrote a special _____ to praise God.

MAKE YOUR CHOICE

To praise God today, I will:

☐ Sing   ☐ Play an instrument

☐ Write a poem or song   ☐ Pray

Thursday — 1 Chronicles 16:23-29

TAKE THE CHALLENGE

We'll never run out of reasons to worship God!

CHECK IT OUT

Find as many words about God as you can in this puzzle!

BEAUTY - FEARED - GLORY
GREAT - HOLY - MAJESTY
PRAISED - SALVATION
SPLENDOR - STRENGTH

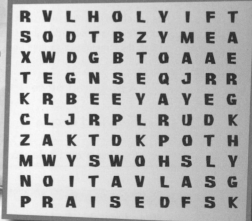

```
R V L H O L Y I F T
S O D T B Z Y M E A
X W D G B T O A A E
T E G N S E Q J R R
K R B E E Y A Y E G
C L J R P L R U D K
Z A K T D K P O T H
M W Y S W O H S L Y
N O I T A V L A S G
P R A I S E D F S K
```

MAKE YOUR CHOICE

I'm excited about how _____ God is!

FRiDAY — 1 Chronicles 17:1-15

TAKE THE CHALLENGE

Do you ever dream of doing great things for God?

CHECK IT OUT:

David dreamed of building a beautiful house for God. Good idea! But God told Nathan the prophet to go tell David that he is _____ the one to build God's _____!'" Check verses 11 and 12 to find out who would build God's house—David's _____.

MAKE YOUR CHOICE

Thank you, God, that You have the "big picture" plan. Help me to see what part of Your plan You want _____ to do.

SATURDAY — 1 Chronicles 17:16-27

TAKE THE CHALLENGE

Did you know that King David had his quiet time with God, too?

CHECK IT OUT:

Complete the phrase from verse 16 that tells us David had a special place to meet with God. David the King came and "_____ _____ _____ _____" Was his prayer mostly praising God or asking for things? _____

MAKE YOUR CHOICE

My special place to sit and talk with God is: _____
_____

chrt yr crrs

David was the KING!—The most important person in Israel—So certainly it was "all about him," right? Read this week to find out what was important to David, and then think about yourself:

Is it better to **get**? Or to **give**?

Is it "All about **me**"? or

All about **GOd** and **Others**?

Sunday 1 Chronicles 21:18-26

TAKE THE CHALLENGE

Does your gift to the Lord cost you anything?

CHECK IT OUT

David needed a place to build an altar. Ornan the Jebusite offered him land, material to build the altar, and animals to sacrifice. What was David's reply in verse 24?

I will pay the _____ _____

I will not take what is _____

I will not offer something to God that costs me

_____

MAKE YOUR CHOICE

What can I give to the Lord? _____

Will it cost me any time, effort, discomfort, or money to give this gift? **Yes / No**

1 Chronicles 22:1-10

TAKE THE CHALLENGE

Think of some things that you have to think through and prepare before you start working on a school project.

CHECK IT OUT

David wasn't going to build the temple, but he was

willing to help prepare for this huge job.

What materials did gather? _____

_____

Who was to build the temple?_____

MAKE YOUR CHOICE

I can help _____ (fill in name) prepare for

_____ (fill in a task or project) even

though it's not my job.

Tuesday 1 Chronicles 22:11-19

TAKE THE CHALLENGE

When you have a huge job, how can you keep from getting tired and discouraged?

CHECK IT OUT

David helped Solomon prepare his heart for this

big job: Verse 12 - David prayed for _____

and _____ for Solomon. Verse 13 - David said

Solomon would have success if he _____

God's laws. Verse 19 - David said Solomon should

devote his heart and soul to _____

the Lord.

MAKE YOUR CHOICE

I can keep from getting discouraged by _____

God every day. I can seek God by reading the _____

_____.

wednesday 1 Chronicles 28:1-10

TAKE THE CHALLENGE

How do you feel when you are chosen for something special?

CHECK IT OUT

What did God choose David to do?_____

What did God choose Judah to do?_____

What did God choose Solomon to do?_____

We don't know why God chose these men, but we do know what advice David gave Solomon at the end of verse 10: "_____

_____." (In other words **"JUST DO IT!"**)

MAKE YOUR CHOICE

No matter what task God chooses me for today, the best thing I can do is _____.

Thursday 1 Chronicles 28:20-29:9

TAKE THE CHALLENGE

Which is better, getting or giving?

CHECK IT OUT

Search for these things the people gave:

BRASS GOLD

IRON STONES

WOOD MARBLE

SILVER THEMSELVES

R	V	S	T	O	N	E	S	F	D
E	O	S	T	B	O	L	M	E	O
V	W	A	G	B	R	B	A	A	O
L	E	R	N	S	I	R	J	R	W
I	R	B	E	E	Y	A	Y	E	G
S	E	V	L	E	S	M	E	H	T
Z	A	O	O	D	L	O	G	T	H

MAKE YOUR CHOICE

I will eagerly look for ways to give my money and myself to the Lord. Some things I can give this week are_____

_____

FRIDAY   1 Chronicles 29:10-19

TAKE THE CHALLENGE

Is it right to be proud of what you give?

CHECK IT OUT

Write the verse number that says these things come from God:

Riches

Honor

Strength

Everything

MAKE YOUR CHOICE

Everything that I GIVE comes from _____.

To Him be the glory when I am blessed to be able to give!

SATURDAY   1 Chronicles 29:20-30

TAKE THE CHALLENGE

What attitude do you have toward your parents, teachers, pastor, and other leaders?

CHECK IT OUT

Write the words from verses 22-25 that tell us how the

people treated Solomon: _____

_____

_____

_____

MAKE YOUR CHOICE

A leader or authority in my life that I need to treat

with more respect is_____

ch
rt
y
r rc
rs

Old Testament Words to Know...

COVENANT means a promise, agreement, or contract.

BURNT OFFERING means burning an animal to symbolize total surrender to God.

ARK means a container.

NOAH'S ARK was a boat containing God's people.

THE ARK OF THE COVENANT was a chest containing a record of God's covenant with His people.

Sunday 2 Chronicles 1:1-12

TAKE THE CHALLENGE

If you could ask for ANYTHING, what would you ask for?

CHECK IT OUT

What did Solomon ask for? _____ and

_____ What did God give Solomon?

Not only _____ and _____,

but also _____, _____, and

_____. Was Solomon selfish or

unselfish in his request? _____

MAKE YOUR CHOICE

A selfish prayer that I have been praying lately is:

_____ . Lord, make my

wants and desires pleasing to you, so I want what You want!

monday

2 Chronicles 5:1-14

TAKE THE CHALLENGE

What do you like to celebrate?

CHECK IT OUT

DOWN
1. In which month was the ark brought to the temple?
2. Name of the City of David
3. The temple of the Lord was filled with what?
4. Name of the tribe that carried the ark
6. Instruments played by 120 priests

ACROSS
5. What the Levite musicians wore
7. The ark was placed under the wings of what?

MAKE YOUR CHOICE

A good thing to celebrate is the goodness of: _____

Tuesday

2 Chronicles 6:1-11

TAKE THE CHALLENGE

Do promises always come true?

CHECK IT OUT

Well... it depends on who makes the promise!
Verse 4 says that God, with His _____,
fulfilled what He said with His _____
"Fulfilled" means _____
(Use a dictionary or ask a grownup.)
Write the words from verse 10 that tell us God did what he said "_____

_____ "

MAKE YOUR CHOICE

Circle the word to make this a true statement:
I know that God   sometimes / often / always
keeps His promises. I can _____ on Him!

147

wednesday   2 Chronicles 6:12-21

What kinds of prayers does God love to answer?

CHECK IT OUT King Solomon prayed for God to:

_____ His promises

_____ his eyes

_____ their prayers

_____ their sins

When I pray, I . . .

	ask for things I want or need		praise and thank God
	pray for people I love		ask God for spiritual help

Thursday   2 Chronicles 6:22-31

Can bad things happen because of sin?

CHECK IT OUT From this passage, list bad things that could happen to

Israel because of their sin:_____

_____

What were the people to do when God used bad things

to show them their sin? (Verse 24)_____

When bad things happen I should check with God to see if I

have any _____ in my life.

FRiDAY — 2 Chronicles 6:32-42

TAKE THE CHALLENGE

What is God's way of dealing with sin?

CHECK IT OUT

Verse 36 - Is there anyone who doesn't sin?_____

Verse 36 - How does God feel about sin?_____

Verse 37 - What words show that the people are sorry for their sin?_____

Verse 39 - What does Solomon ask God to do if they turn away from their sin?_____

MAKE YOUR CHOICE

Thank you, God, for Your forgiving heart. Help me to
_____ away from sin.

SATURDAY — 2 Chronicles 7:1-11

TAKE THE CHALLENGE

Is God pleased with your worship?

CHECK IT OUT

What position were the people in when the fire came down?_____ What position were they in when the priests blew their trumpets?_____

_____ What was the attitude of their hearts after they worshiped? _____

and _____

MAKE YOUR CHOICE

In my worship, I will remember that God is more concerned about: ☐ How I sit or stand ☐ How I look

☐ What my attitude is like

149

34

2 Chronicles 7:12-20:30

God's people are easily *DISTRACTED*.

This week we will see how they are distracted from God by sin, difficult circumstances, idols, riches, and enemies. We will also see what it takes to stay FOCUSED on God so we can have His best!

Sunday   2 Chronicles 7:12-22

TAKE THE CHALLENGE

Is there a secret formula for maintaining a great relationship with God?

CHECK IT OUT

Match each phrase from verse 14 with its meaning to see four important things God wants His people to do.

- Humble themselves
- Pray
- Seek My face
- Turn from their wicked ways

- Talk to God
- Repent
- Don't be proud
- Look for God's direction in His Word

MAKE YOUR CHOICE

Even if there is no magic formula, I want to do everything God says in order to stay close to Him! (Mark anything above that you need to work on today.)

monday
2 Chronicles 9:1-14

TAKE THE CHALLENGE

Have you ever heard of the Queen of Sheba? (She sounds royal and exotic!)

CHECK IT OUT

Mark an X by each thing that the queen did while visiting Solomon

- [ ] Tested him with hard questions
- [ ] Gave him costly gifts
- [ ] Tried to hurt him
- [ ] Praised God for how He had blessed Solomon
- [ ] Stole from him

MAKE YOUR CHOICE

When God blesses me, I should use this as an opportunity to:

_____ Brag about the good things I have

_____ Give testimony to others about how good God is

Tuesday
2 Chronicles 9:15-31

TAKE THE CHALLENGE

What is your drinking cup made out of?

CHECK IT OUT

Solomon's drinking vessels were made of _____ _____ !

Search for other possessions that Solomon owned

ANIMALS   CHARIOTS

HORSES   IVORY   ROBES

SILVER   SPICES

P	O	I	K	S	S	S	Q	L	W
Q	Z	F	V	J	Y	B	G	M	I
Z	L	E	M	O	B	X	S	C	D
X	B	H	A	E	R	P	P	H	W
S	I	L	V	E	R	Y	I	A	R
A	N	I	M	A	L	S	C	R	O
S	E	S	R	O	H	A	E	I	B
J	U	K	N	T	A	P	S	O	E
H	U	I	Q	M	I	O	A	T	S
M	Y	A	R	K	W	Q	F	S	F

MAKE YOUR CHOICE

God, help me to have the right attitude toward Your blessings, and be _____ for all the material possessions you entrust me with.

wednesday
2 Chronicles 12:5-16

TAKE THE CHALLENGE

What is your reaction when bad things happen?

CHECK IT OUT

What was the name of the bad king that God used to punish Israel? (See verses 2 & 5.)_____
What was the reaction of the leaders when they heard God was going to let them be punished?

a. They _____ themselves.

b. They said the Lord is _____.

Because of their right response, what did God do?

_____

MAKE YOUR CHOICE

When bad things happen (especially because of my own sin) I should:

☐ Panic ☐ Whine & Complain ☐ Scream & Yell

☐ Acknowledge that God is always right, and trust Him

Thursday
2 Chronicles 15:1-15

TAKE THE CHALLENGE

Did you know..... you are as close to God as you choose to be?

CHECK IT OUT

Match these phrases according to today's scripture:

_____ 1.If you seek him   **A. He will forsake you**

_____ 2. If you are with him   **B. You will find him**

_____ 3. If you forsake him   **C. He is with you**

Under King Asa, did Judah seek the Lord?_____
Did they find him?_____ What did He give
them?_____ all around them — on every side.

MAKE YOUR CHOICE

I will seek God every day in the _____
(what time of the day do you have your Quiet Time?) and
by talking to Him through _____.

FRIDAY 2 Chronicles 20:1-13

TAKE THE

What do you do when you come up against a very difficult task or problem?

CHECK IT OUT

Where did Jehoshaphat look for help when the huge army was coming?_____

Write out Jehoshaphat's prayer (v. 12) in the box below:

_____

_____

_____

In verse 13, what kinds of people stood before the Lord in prayer? _____

MAKE YOUR CHOICE

My big problem right now is: _____

_____ and I don't

know what to do about it! I will keep my eyes on _____

SATURDAY 2 Chronicles 20:14-30

TAKE THE CHALLENGE

So how did Jehoshaphat's prayer get answered?

CHECK IT OUT

ACROSS
3. God gave them _____ roundabout (on all sides).
4. God said, "Be not (do not be) _____."
5. As they set out they began to sing and _____ God.

DOWN
1. What the people did in verse 18
2. The big army started to destroy each _____

MAKE YOUR CHOICE

Thank you, God, for this example of how You _____ Your people when they _____ You.

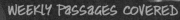
What do you know about the monstrous King Ahaz? Did you know ...he was a very wicked King? ...he ruled in Judah for sixteen years? ...that during his reign, he led the nation in worshiping idols, making human sacrifices, going to enemy nations for help, and shutting the doors of the temple of God? ...that when he died, the nation of Judah was far from God?

Sunday   2 Chronicles 29:1-11

TAKE THE CHALLENGE Can one person make a difference?

CHECK IT OUT

Match these facts about King Hezekiah by drawing lines between them.

His character

His first act as king

His leadership

His confession

His commitment

He opened and repaired the doors of the temple.

He brought together the priests and Levites.

He did what was right in the eyes of the Lord.

"I will make a covenant with God."

"Our fathers were unfaithful."

MAKE YOUR CHOICE

I want to make a difference in (circle your choices, or fill in your own answer): **My school   My family   My ball team   My Sunday school class   My neighborhood** _____

2 Chronicles 29:27-36

TAKE THE CHALLENGE   What is the best way to celebrate?

Worship God!

CHECK IT OUT

Write the verse number where you find the different things that Hezekiah's people did in worship.

☐	Offered sacrifices
☐	Sang
☐	Played instrument
☐	Read psalms written by David and Asaph
☐	Bowed or knelt
☐	Brought offerings

MAKE YOUR CHOICE

I want to be excited about worshiping God! Put a check mark beside the ways listed above that show how I can worship Him this week.

2 Chronicles 30:1-12

TAKE THE CHALLENGE   Do you learn from seeing others make mistakes?

CHECK IT OUT

Hezekiah's letter warned them NOT to be like their ancestors! What word in verse 8 means stubborn?

_____-_____ Hezekiah's advice?

_____ the Lord _____ to the Lord

MAKE YOUR CHOICE

I am:

a. Always right, never wrong.

b. Willing to admit my mistakes and learn from them.

wednesday · 2 Chronicles 30:18-27

TAKE THE CHALLENGE

Which is more important – actions or attitudes?

CHECK IT OUT

The people didn't follow every rule about how to eat the Passover, but Hezekiah asked for forgiveness because their _____ were set on seeking God. Did God answer this prayer?_____ Later, how many priests purified themselves (v. 24)?

_____

MAKE YOUR CHOICE

God, help me to follow Your rules, but more importantly, to seek You with all my _____

Thursday · 2 Chronicles 33:1-10

TAKE THE CHALLENGE

A new King! And only 12 years old!

CHECK IT OUT

The king's name was _____.

Was he a good king or a bad king?_____

Did he pay attention when the Lord spoke to him?

_____

MAKE YOUR CHOICE

When God shows me I am wrong about something, I:
_____ Ignore Him and keep doing "my own thing"
_____ Stop. Repent. Do right.

FRIDAY — 2 Chronicles 33:11-19

TAKE THE CHALLENGE

Has God ever used bad people to get your attention?

CHECK IT OUT

Manasseh didn't listen to God, so....

What country took him prisoner?_____

Where did they take him?_____

When he was in bad trouble, THEN he acknowledged God!! What did God do then?_____

What did Manasseh do then?_____

MAKE YOUR CHOICE

God, help me to listen to You all the time so You don't have to use _____ to get my attention.

SATURDAY — 2 Chronicles 36:11-21

TAKE THE CHALLENGE

How many chances does God give us to "get it right"?

CHECK IT OUT

Find two phrases in verse 13 that tell us King Zedekiah was stubborn. His neck was _____ His heart was _____ Many times God sent messengers because he cared greatly for His people. How did they treat God's messengers?_____ them. Because they ignored God's warnings, God's people were killed or carried away to what country?

_____

MAKE YOUR CHOICE

I _____ want to be guilty of ignoring God and taking advantage of His great patience.

36

1 Peter 1:1-3:7

ΙΧΘΥΣ

Did you know that early Christians used the fish symbol like a secret code? When fish is spelled in the Greek language, its letters form the initials (called an acrostic) of the phrase: "Jesus Christ, God's Son, Savior."

Sunday   1 Peter 1:1-8

TAKE THE CHALLENGE

Have you ever sensed Jesus' presence with you when you went through a rough time in your life or family?

Finish the letter below from today's part of Peter's letter or epistle.

CHECK IT OUT

Dear Friends who live all over P_____, G_____, Cappadocia, A_____ and Bithynia. All of you have been chosen ("elect") according to the _____ of God, and the sanctifying work ("sanctification") of the _____. Praise (blessed) be to the God and _____ of Jesus Who has given us living hope through the r_____ of Jesus Christ from the d_____ to an eternal heavenly inheritance. Wherein ("in this") you greatly r_____ . . . because the trial (test) of your faith (v. 7), being more valuable than g_____ . . . may result in ("be found in") _____ and _____ and _____ at Jesus' second coming.

Sincerely Yours, (v. 1)

_____, an _____ of _____ _____

YOUR CHOICE

One hard thing I am going through lately is _____

What is one way I could see my faith in God grow stronger? _____

_____

monday
1 Peter 1:9-16

TAKE THE CHALLENGE

Can you believe that God's very angels do not understand the salvation in Christ we enjoy? (Check out verses 9-12!)

CHECK IT OUT

When you begin doing the teen Quiet Time Diary, one of the things you are to look for, in order to make the passage applicable to your life, is this: "Is there a command I need to obey in this passage?" Well, in verses 13-16, there are at least four commands we need to obey. Write them here: v. 13a - _____

v. 13b - _____(serious minded)

v. 13c - _____

v. 16 – (You shall) "Be ye _____, for (because) I (God) am _____."

MAKE YOUR CHOICE

I can be like God today if I live a _____ life. One area in which I can be holy is: _____

_____

Tuesday
1 Peter 1:17-25

TAKE THE CHALLENGE

How much do you really know about your Savior, Jesus?

CHECK IT OUT

In verses 17-21, we can see lots of special things about Jesus Christ if we look closely. Circle the things below that these verses tell us about our Savior:

His blood redeemed us

Baptized by John

Lion of Judah

Glorified by the Father

Lamb without blemish or sin

Chosen before creation

Judge of all sinners

Revealed or manifest in these last times for us

MAKE YOUR CHOICE

If Jesus loved me so much that He shed His life's blood for my redemption, then I need to have sincere _____ for my Christian _____. How can I prove Jesus' love to someone else today? _____

_____

wednesday — 1 Peter 2:1-10

TAKE THE CHALLENGE

Have you ever seen a newborn baby when he is hungry? What does he want?

CHECK IT OUT

What do new born Christians need to eat so they can grow in their faith? (v. 1) If I ever feel insecure or like a nobody, I can remember that, as part of God's family, I am what four things? (See verse 9.)

1. _____
2. _____
3._____
4, _____

Wow! I'm special to God!

MAKE YOUR CHOICE

How do I know I am special to God? _____
_____

Thursday — 1 Peter 2:11-17

TAKE THE CHALLENGE

Have you ever encountered an alien being? How would you know an alien if you saw one?

CHECK IT OUT

What are we believers in this world, according to verse 11? _____
and _____ As an alien or pilgrim, I need to _____ from
_____ that _____ against my
_____. People around me who aren't Christians need to see my good be-
havior and _____ God. What are four commands given to us in verse 17?

☐ (1) _____
☐ (2)_____
☐ (3)_____
☐ (4)_____

MAKE YOUR CHOICE

If I was tried in court for being a Christian - a Heaven-bound alien - would I be convicted based on my deeds and words? YES / NO

FRIDAY

1 Peter 2:18-25

TAKE THE CHALLENGE

Have you ever worn a WWJD (What Would Jesus Do?) bracelet on your wrist? What did it remind you to do?

CHECK IT OUT

Can you find these five things Jesus is (from our verses for today) in the word puzzle?

SINLESS, EXAMPLE, SINBEARER, SHEPHERD, OVERSEER (This word, by the way, means Bishop.)

```
S N X C M Y R T A L O
I E X A M P L E E D R
N Z Q D H T L M N Y E
B S I N L E S S E D E
E N C L E A N B R O S
A E O I U J O E V X R
R R P F H S H N M O E
E L A E I P U A G E V
R U R D E R B A X V O
L J H H D T Y E O L K
L J S N D T Y E O L K
```

MAKE YOUR CHOICE

I can follow Christ's example of holiness by asking, "W_____ W_____ J_____ D____?" before I do or say anything.

SATURDAY

1 Peter 3:1-7

TAKE THE CHALLENGE

Have you ever wondered how you will know the right person to marry some day?

CHECK IT OUT

This passage speaks to both husbands and wives. God defines what truly makes a beautiful wife or woman in verses 2-6. Cross out (with an X) the things below that don't fit into God's description.

pure   nice clothes   submissive

great hairstyle   gentle   reverent

expensive jewelry   godly   quiet   thin

and fit   obedient   make-up on

MAKE YOUR CHOICE

Describe, in one sentence, some qualities I will look for in my future mate: _____

_____

1 Peter 3:8-5:14

c h rt y r c rs

Peter speaks to suffering Christians everywhere. Did you know that . . .

~ Many Christians in other countries, even our own, stand up for Jesus in the face of awful kinds of persecution and even death?

~ Those who die for their faith are called martyrs.

~ Every three minutes a believer somewhere in the world is being tortured or killed for their faith in Jesus Christ?

HERE LIES:
Believer who died

Sunday   1 Peter 3:8-12

TAKE THE CHALLENGE

Have you ever been really sick, and when you went to the doctor, he wrote out a prescription for you to take so you could get well?

CHECK IT OUT

Peter gives two godly prescriptions in these verses. Finish filling out the prescription scripts. Diagonosis: **DISUNITY - RX for a life of UNITY** — How to live in harmony ("one mind"): Love like brothers +

Be _____ _____ +Be _____ + Don't repay, render or return _____ for _____ or _____ for _____ but rather a b_____. Diagnosis: **A SAD LIFE - RX for a LOVING LIFE** — How to "love life and see good days!": Keep (refrain) your _____ from _____ + Keep your _____ from deceitful speech or guile + Turn away from or eschew _____ +Seek _____ and _____ it.

MAKE YOUR CHOICE

Circle three things above I need to work on. What kind of life do I want to have? _____
_____

monday

1 Peter 3:13-18

TAKE THE CHALLENGE

When was the last time you tried to tell someone about Christ and salvation, but you didn't know how to stand against their false arguments?

CHECK IT OUT

Peter says here that we can even be a witness for Christ when unfair things or hardships are happening to us. But, in order to be an effective witness to the unsaved around us, verse 15 tells us we must: (1) Sanctify or set apart Christ as Lord in our _____. (2) Always be _____ to give an answer to those who want to know the reason for the _____ that is in us, as Christians. (3) Make sure you we share the truth of the gospel message — the Answer — with what two attitudes? _____ and _____

MAKE YOUR CHOICE

According to verse 18, Christ suffered and died for my _____ to bring me to _____. If Christ died for me, surely I can tell _____ about His love and salvation.

Tuesday   1 Peter 4:1-6

TAKE THE CHALLENGE

What were your attitudes and actions like before you came to know Jesus as your Savior from sin?

CHECK IT OUT

When Christ died on the cross, He died to pay for all our sins. Before we have Christ's life and become His children, we are spiritually dead in our sins, and our sins separate us from God. The coffin below represents a person who is spiritually dead. Look at verse 3 and list on the blank lines five terrible sins these Christians (to whom Peter was writing) had once been involved in as unsaved (dead in sins) people.

DEAD IN SINS

_____

_____   _____

_____   _____

MAKE YOUR CHOICE

Before I became a Christian, I was _____.

Now I am _____.

163

wednesday 1 Peter 4:7-11

What would you want to be doing if Jesus was to come back today?

CHECK IT OUT

Peter tells believers here that the _____ of all things is _____! Write down any two things he tells us to be doing, in light of Christ's soon (imminent) return:

(1) _____

(2) _____

MAKE YOUR CHOICE

No matter what we do or how we do it, it should all be done so that God may be _____ through _____.
To Whom / Him be (belongs) _____ and _____ forever and ever. _____. (v.11b)

Thursday 1 Peter 4:12-19

TAKE THE CHALLENGE

What do you think it would be like to truly suffer for Jesus? Have you ever suffered hardships in Jesus' name?

CHECK IT OUT

We Christians are not to be surprised or think it a strange thing concerning the _____ _____ that we might be suffering through. Instead, Peter encourages us to _____ in our trials, because we get to participate or share in the very sufferings of _____.
If we get to share in Christ's sufferings, then someday, when His glory is revealed, we will also get to share in His _____. That will be the best kind of joy!

MAKE YOUR CHOICE

Look at verse 19. If I ever have the opportunity to _____ according to the _____ of _____, I should obediently commit myself — my life — to my
f_____ C_____.

FRIDAY
1 Peter 5:1-7

TAKE THE CHALLENGE

Do you ever think that one day you might be a leader, Sunday school teacher, or pastor in the church? Your preparation begins now!

CHECK IT OUT

After Peter explains how pastors or church leaders should shepherd the believers in their care, he tells us younger believers to prepare for godly leadership in certain ways. Match the phrase that completes his advice below. (Put the letter of the correct answer in the blank next to its match.)

_____ Cast all your care/anxiety

_____ Be subject or submissive

_____ Humble yourselves

_____ Clothe/gird yourselves

_____ God opposes or resists

_____ To the humble

A. To your elders or older believers

B. The proud

C. God gives grace

D. With humility

E. Under God's mighty hand

F. Upon Him (God)

MAKE YOUR CHOICE

Can I think of one person who has a humble spirit or attitude? Yes / No

Write their name here: _____

What is there about this person's example of humility that I can follow?

SATURDAY
1 Peter 5:8-14

TAKE THE CHALLENGE

What do you do when Satan (the old trickster that he is) tries to tempt you to do wrong or turn from God's Word?

CHECK IT OUT

Circle each and every thing these verses tell us to do in order to beat the devil at his sinful "game." He is called a _____ _____ here

Be sober / Run / Stand firm in the faith

Be self-controlled and alert! / Resist him

Act like you don't know he's there / Be steadfast

Stand fast in God's grace / Hide!

Go ahead and sin / Scream out loud!

MAKE YOUR CHOICE

I will be victorious over the devil and his tricks today by . . .

_____

_____ !

WEEKLY PASSAGES COVERED
Exodus 1:1—4:17

EX is a prefix meaning *out of*. Think of all the many words that start with ex . . .

Exit, Extra, Exemplary, Example, Execute, Excite, Excuse, Explain AND of course, EXODUS!

We will be starting on a long, adventurous journey with Moses this week. By the way, "exodus" means "a going out." It is the story of Israel's big exit from Egypt. When Joseph's family moved to Egypt, there were 70 Israelites. Now, almost 400 years later, they had multiplied to over 500,000 Jews! Half a MILLION!

Sunday — Exodus 1:1-14

TAKE THE CHALLENGE

Have you ever been hired to do a job where you get paid for it? How would you like to work all day in the hot sun for nothing?

CHECK IT OUT

How were the children of Israel being treated by the new Pharaoh (king) and the Egyptian slave masters (v. 11)? _____

_____

"But the more they afflicted (oppressed) them the more they _____ and _____." (v. 12).

MAKE YOUR CHOICE

Sometimes God allows us to go through hard and unfair things so that He can help us grow and mature in His grace. What is something in my life that feels really unfair right now? _____

Am I willing to grow through this? **Yes / No**

Exodus 1:15-22

TAKE THE CHALLENGE

Girls, how would you like a name like Shiphrah or Puah? Sort of strange, huh? We'll see in today's passage how these Egyptian gals were used of God!

CHECK IT OUT

The Egyptian king wanted all the _____ babies killed at birth. He was tired of the Israelites multiplying in his land! Do you think the midwives (baby delivery nurses) should have obeyed Pharaoh since he was the leader? **Yes / No** Why not? _____

_____

How did God reward these Egyptian midwives who saved the lives of the little baby boys (v. 21)?

_____

MAKE YOUR CHOICE

The Apostle Peter in the New Testament once said, "I must obey GOD rather than MEN." If someone instructs me to do something wrong that is against God's commands, I should always obey _____ over what humans say.

Tuesday Exodus 2:1-10

TAKE THE CHALLENGE

Have you ever had to watch or take care of your little brother or sister for awhile while Mom was busy? Were you responsible?

CHECK IT OUT

Today we read about two more females who were very important! Who were they? _____'s

_____ and Moses' _____

When the Princess of Egypt came down to the Nile River to wash up, what did she find there (v. 6)?

_____ The name "Moses" means drawn or pulled out. Why did Pharaoh's daughter give the baby that name? _____

MAKE YOUR CHOICE

Just think, what might have happened if Moses' big sister had left him by himself or not really watched him? His mother would have never known what happened to him! I will be _____ and _____ when I am given the care of someone.

167

wednesday Exodus 2:11-25

TAKE THE CHALLENGE

Have you ever made a bad choice or decision that later ended up putting you in a place or situation where God could teach you an important lesson you may not have learned otherwise?

CHECK IT OUT

What really awful choice did Moses make in this story? _____ Where did Moses run to escape (250 miles away!)? _____ What did God give him as a result of his living and working in this desert area? A _____ named Z_____ and a s_____ named G_____. What four things did God do (vv. 24-25) when the suffering Jews cried out to Him? 1- He _____ them. 2- He r_____ His promise to their forefathers. 3- He looked on (saw) them. 4-He _____ _____ .

MAKE YOUR CHOICE

When I make a choice that hurts me as well as others, I can confess my sin to God and ask Him to teach me and help me in the future. I know God _____ me when I cry out to Him, and I know He _____.

Thursday Exodus 3:1-12

TAKE THE CHALLENGE

Have you ever seen a forest fire burning? It is a really frightening thing!

CHECK IT OUT

One day out in the Midian wilderness, Moses spied a _____ _____ - probably a mimosa or thorny acacia tree. It really wasn't unusual to see a bush on fire in the hot, dry desert. But the UNUSUAL thing about this burning tree was that it didn't _____ up!   What assignment did God give Moses here? (See verse 10.)

MAKE YOUR CHOICE

Would I do exactly what God told me if He talked to me out of a burning bush? Yes / No Then why don't I do exactly what He tells me in His living WORD each day?

FRIDAY — Exodus 3:13-22

TAKE THE CHALLENGE

Do you ever question God? Do you wonder if He's for real?

CHECK IT OUT

Moses answers God's instruction out of the burning bush with a question today. He asks God what His _____ is (end of verse 13). How does God answer this very important question? "I _____ _____ _____ _____." What other names did He identify Himself as to Moses in verse 15?

(1)_____ (2)_____

(3)_____ (4)_____

MAKE YOUR CHOICE

It's not a sin for me to question God. If I share my doubts with Him, honestly wanting to know Him and know more about Him, He will reveal Himself to me! What is a question I've had about God? _____
NOW ASK GOD about that!

SATURDAY — Exodus 4:1-17

TAKE THE CHALLENGE

Do you ever make excuses for not doing what you've been asked to do? Maybe it sounds like this: "Mom, I can't empty the trash right now! My favorite cartoons are on!" Sound familiar?

CHECK IT OUT

What are two excuses Moses made in today's dialogue with God (involving a _____ that turned into a s_____ of all things!)? (1) What if _____
_____(v. 1)?

(2) I'm not good at _____
(v. 10). Moses had a speech problem. He probably stuttered. It's good God sent his _____,
A_____ (v. 14), to help him out.

MAKE YOUR CHOICE

Someday God may want to call me to be a Christian leader, pastor, missionary, or Sunday school teacher. How can I be prepared to say "Yes" to God with no excuses when that time comes? _____

WEEKLY PASSAGES COVERED
Exodus 4:18–8:15

Did you know . . .

That when Moses was educated in the Pharaoh's palace as a prince, his course of instruction would have been geometry, poetry, hieroglyphics, and astronomy? . . . That Moses ran about 250 miles to get to Midian after he murdered the Egyptian worker? . . . That the "bulrushes" baby Moses was hidden in were actually 3-sided reeds that grew up to 16 feet tall and were made into 120 feet long rolls of paper (papyrus)?

Sunday   Exodus 4:27-31

TAKE THE CHALLENGE

Can you think of anything the heavenly Father has done for you this week that reminds you of His love and care?

CHECK IT OUT

Who did the Lord tell Aaron to go into the desert to meet? _____ What did Moses tell his older brother about after he kissed him? _____

_____

_____Then what did Aaron tell all the Israelite leaders (v. 30)? _____

_____ Did they believe it?

Yes / No

MAKE YOUR CHOICE

In verse 31, when the leaders of Israel realized that God was truly concerned about them, what did they do? " _____
" What do I need to do today when I remember how much God loves and cares for me? _____

Exodus 5:1-12

TAKE THE CHALLENGE

People don't always respond to us like we wish they would, do they?

CHECK IT OUT

When Moses and Aaron went the first time to Pharaoh to ask him to "_____ my _____!", Pharaoh arrogantly told them (v. 2b), "I _____ _____." Then what did he do out of spite to make it even harder for the Israelite slaves (vv. 9-12)?_____ _____

MAKE YOUR CHOICE

Sometimes when we do the will of God, things do not always go so smoothly at first. We must trust God and keep doing what He's called us to do! Who have I been witnessing to or trying to be a testimony to about God, and they are unkind to me or make fun? _____ Don't give up!

Tuesday

Exodus 5:13-23

TAKE THE CHALLENGE

When's the last time you felt misunderstood? Not a fun feeling, is it?

CHECK IT OUT

When the Israelite leaders went to Pharaoh to complain, he called them _____ (v. 17) and told them they still had to meet the same quota of _____ with less materials. Who did the leaders complain to (vv. 20-21)? _____ and _____ Who did Moses go back and complain or cry out to? The _____

MAKE YOUR CHOICE

Sometimes godly leaders are misunderstood when they try to accomplish what God has called them to do. Am I willing to be misunderstood by others for Jesus' sake — to fulfill His will for my life? Yes / No

wednesday — Exodus 6:1-13

TAKE THE CHALLENGE

What is your favorite sport? To be a good player in that sport, do you have to keep at it? Do you have to trust your coach?

CHECK IT OUT

God encourages fearful Moses here with lots of "I WILLS . . ."! Circle all the things God says He will do:

"I WILL" .. Do bad things to Pharaoh   *Bring you out*

Will free you   *Will deliver you*

Rid you out of their bondage   *Make you really rich*

Redeem you   **Take you for my own people**

BE YOUR GOD   Teach you how to read

Bring you into the land   Give it to you

MAKE YOUR CHOICE

When I can't, GOD WILL! What would I like to ask God to do for me that seems impossible right now? _____
_____ ***Now ASK Him!***

Thursday — Exodus 6:28–7:13

TAKE THE CHALLENGE

Remember that staff (stick) that turned into a snake? Well, look for it again today!

CHECK IT OUT

What excuse does Moses use today when God tells him to tell Pharaoh everything He has been telling him (v. 30)?
"_____"

What did God ultimately want the Egyptians to know (v. 5)? _____

How do you know Aaron was older than Moses? _____
_____ What did Aaron's snake-staff do to the magician's snake-sticks? _____

MAKE YOUR CHOICE

One of the Egyptian gods, Nechebt, was represented by a cobra snake. But God's snake won, didn't it? How is God winning in my life over the "serpent," Satan's, attempts to get me to make sinful choices in my life? _____

172

FRIDAY — Exodus 7:14-25

TAKE THE CHALLENGE

Do you know what a plague is? It is a terrible occurrence that brings death and destruction to a large population of people.

CHECK IT OUT

In the next few chapters, we'll see God put "teeth" in His challenge to Pharaoh, through Moses and Aaron, to let His people GO! He would bring ten different plagues on the Egyptians before Pharaoh would finally give in. Many, many people and animals would die. Each of the plagues targeted a different Egyptian god, showing God's supreme power. This first plague was: _____.

This one was against the deity called "Hapi," the "giver of life." The Nile River was what gave life to their nation.

MAKE YOUR CHOICE

God is MY "g_____ of l_____." His Son's blood flowed to give me new _____ in Him!

SATURDAY — Exodus 8:1-15

TAKE THE CHALLENGE

Do you like catching frogs, or are you afraid of how they feel when you touch them?

CHECK IT OUT

What was the second plague the Lord sent on Egypt today? _____

What does verse 14 tell us about this yucky plague?

_____

_____

How would you like to sleep, eat, shower, and step on frogs, frogs, and more frogs?

MAKE YOUR CHOICE

The frog represented the god, Hekt and the goddess, Hathor. This was not a fun way for God to get their attention. Has God ever had to do something I didn't like or want to get my attention? Yes / No   What was it? _____

_____

173

40

thirtyXrcrs

DID YOU KNOW . . .

That the plagues were a clear, but painful, way for Pharaoh and the Egyptians to get to know about the true God? . . . That the Egyptians worshiped many gods – gods of the river, the sun, the sky, and the crops? . . . That the ten plagues showed the Egyptians that the Living God had more power than all their so-called "gods" put together!?

Sunday   Exodus 8:16-32

TAKE THE CHALLENGE

Have you ever been swarmed by a group of gnats, mosquitoes, or flies? What did it make you want to do?

CHECK IT OUT

What were the third and fourth plagues we see God sending on Egypt today? (vv. 16, 21)

Third: _____ (By the way, these little bugs were stinging insects!) Fourth:

_____ (These insects swarmed around the cattle.) Both of these plagues were judgments against the highly revered goddess, Isis, represented by the cow.

MAKE YOUR CHOICE

If only Pharaoh had given in to God! How often do I refuse to do what God tells me in His Word? _____

What do I need to surrender to Him that is causing a problem in my life? _____

 **Exodus 9:1-12**

TAKE THE CHALLENGE

Have you ever had a boil or oozing sore on your body? It's really painful, and yucky too.

CHECK IT OUT

OK! Let's have a little review today. See if you can number in order the plagues we've seen God bring on the stubborn Egyptians (including the fifth and sixth plagues in today's passage). There may be one or two thrown in just to confuse you! ____ Frogs ____ Tsunami ____ Lice or gnats ____ Water to blood ____ Animal and cattle disease ____ Swarming flies ____ Boils [By the way, the cattle disease was aimed against Ptah, represented by a bull. And the boils were targeted against the Egyptian temple priests who kept themselves so clean all the time!]

MAKE YOUR CHOICE

The boils remind us of Job in the Bible, who had boils all over his body, but still trusted God to deliver him. Sometimes we have "HEART-sores" that we need to let God heal. Is there a deep hurt in my heart that I need God to heal? _____

Tuesday **Exodus 9:13-26**

TAKE THE CHALLENGE

When's the last time you saw it hail during a big storm? Did you go out and pick it up?

CHECK IT OUT

Today we see a new development! Look at verses 20-21. SOME of Pharaoh's servants or officials actually "_____ _____." But others did what? _____ The seventh plague was a terrible _____ storm. It came down in the fields on both _____ and _____ (v. 25). Hail again insulted Isis, the goddess of life.

MAKE YOUR CHOICE

Do I fear the Lord and trust His Word, or do I harden my heart toward Him when I don't like what He says? _____
Can you make this commitment today: "Today I will listen to God and do one thing that I know He tells me to do in His Word. I will _____."

wednesday   Exodus 9:27-35

TAKE THE CHALLENGE

Who has made a promise to you that was never Kept?

CHECK IT OUT

What did Pharaoh tell Moses he would do if Moses would pray and ask God to stop the horrible hail storms (vv. 27-28)? _____

_____

After the storm stopped, what did Pharaoh and his officials do again? _____

MAKE YOUR CHOICE

What have I ever promised God or my parents that I didn't keep? _____

What will I do about that?? _____

Thursday   Exodus 10:1-15

TAKE THE CHALLENGE

Have you ever heard of an insect that can strip a whole country of all its crops in a matter of hours? Well read on!

CHECK IT OUT

The eighth plague: _____

These were ravenously hungry grasshoppers! They ate everything in sight! What does the last sentence in verse 15 tell us remained to eat? _____

Perhaps this was against Osiris, god of the dead.

MAKE YOUR CHOICE

After seeing what the Egyptians faced because of their stubborn, hard hearts, what do I want to ask God to never let me become? _____

Pray and ask him that right now!

176

FRIDAY — Exodus 10:16-29

TAKE THE CHALLENGE

Has the power ever gone off in your house and left you all in total darkness? Imagine the whole nation being without power – in total darkness! Scary thought, huh?

CHECK IT OUT

The ninth plague the Lord sent was targeted against Ra, the Egyptian sun god. This plague brought total _____ for _____ whole days! But in verse 23 it tells us that all the children of Israel had _____ in their dwellings or homes. Can you imagine this?

MAKE YOUR CHOICE

God has called me to be a light in the darkened, sinful world I live in. Remember Jesus' words, "YOU are the light of the world!"? How am I doing at shining out Jesus' light to others who don't know Him?

_____

SATURDAY — Exodus 11:1-10

TAKE THE CHALLENGE

Pharaoh pushed it all the way to the limits! See what the hardness of his stubborn, sinful heart was going to do to every family in his nation.

CHECK IT OUT

What did Moses tell Pharaoh the tenth and final plague would be (v. 5)? _____ Did this change his mind? _____ ~ Below are listed all the plagues God brought. Unscramble them and write each on the line provided. ETHAD FO NORBRSTIF _____ ____ _____ REWTA OT BOODL _____ ____ _____

LECI _____ LAIH _____ SFLEI _____ RFSGO _____

OLISB _____ TTCAEL SIDESEA _____ _____

CSTUSOL _____ NESSKRAD _____

MAKE YOUR CHOICE

A lot of times when I don't obey God, it affects the lives of others around me. Who might my sin or disobedience negatively influence or affect? _____

177

WEEKLY PASSAGES COVERED
Exodus 12:1–14:14

ch rt y r c rs

DID YOU KNOW . . .

That 600,000 men left Egypt? . . . That counting their wives and children, the count would have risen to 2 ½ to 3 million Jews? . . . That if all those who left were standing in a line, they would stretch from Egypt to the Promised Land and back? . . . That the trip, which should have only taken two to three months, to make, instead took them 40 years? Hard to believe, huh??

Sunday Exodus 12:1-13

TAKE THE CHALLENGE

As you read the account of the Israelites' deliverance from the terrible Death Angel, see if anything reminds you of what Jesus did for you.

CHECK IT OUT

If the Israelites (or even any believing _____) obeyed God by killing a healthy _____ and brushing its _____ on their _____, their _____ _____ would not be killed. The lamb had to die for the firstborn. How is Jesus like this lamb? Look up John 1:29. What did John the Baptist refer to Jesus as in this verse? "Behold, the _____ of God, which taketh away the _____ of the _____."

MAKE YOUR CHOICE

What did the "Lamb of God" do to save me from dying and going to hell?

_____

Who can I tell about His salvation today? _____

monday — Exodus 12:14-24

TAKE THE CHALLENGE

Does your church have Communion Services? What are you supposed to remember when you take Communion?

CHECK IT OUT

God asked the Israelites to celebrate this day in their history, when they were freed from Egypt and Pharaoh. The feast was called the "Feast of _____ _____" because they did not have time to let their bread rise when they fled Egypt. Today it is called the Passover, because it is the time the Death Angel passed over their homes and spared their firstborn sons.

MAKE YOUR CHOICE

Jesus asked Christians to observe a special feast built around His death on Calvary (so that our sin could be forgiven and passed over.) It is called _____. When I eat the little piece of bread it reminds me of His _____, which was broken and bruised for me on the _____. The grape juice reminds me of His _____, which was shed for my sin.

Tuesday — Exodus 12:25-36

Check it out! Tough Pharaoh FINALLY gives in!

TAKE THE CHALLENGE

CHECK IT OUT

Write out Pharaoh's emotional words after all the firstborn in his land had been killed, including his own firstborn son. "_____
_____
_____"

Verse 36 tells us that as the Israelites were getting out, the _____ gave them whatever they asked for just to get rid of them!

MAKE YOUR CHOICE

Am I ready to go wherever God asks me to go — whenever He tells me to? Look back at the end of verse 27 and see what God's people did before they left? _____ and _____ God Have you ever gotten down on your knees (bowed) and told God how much you love Him? Try it!

179

wednesday — Exodus 12:37-51

TAKE THE CHALLENGE What's the longest you've ever lived in one house or one place?

CHECK IT OUT

How long had the Israelites been living in Egypt? _____ years   After God explained the Passover feast to His people, all of them did just what the _____ had _____ Moses and _____. And on that very day, the Lord brought them _____ of _____! Hurray! Finally!

MAKE YOUR CHOICE

Who is the only One Who can bring me out of the place of bondage, sin and darkness? _____
What did He free ME from when I trusted Christ as my Savior? _____

Thursday — Exodus 13:1-10

TAKE THE CHALLENGE Today you will see the word "sanctify" or "consecrate." That word simply means "to separate or set apart for God's glory and use."

CHECK IT OUT

All of the animals and children that were born first in each family were to be set apart to God so that the Israelites would remember the _____ from which God had _____ them. Circle **T** for true and **F** for false statements: **T / F** The unleavened bread was to be eaten 3 days a year. **T / F** They were going to a land of milk and honey. **T / F** Every firstborn female was to be consecrated to God.

MAKE YOUR CHOICE

What in my life do I need to consecrate or set apart to God alone? _____

FRIDAY   Exodus 13:11-22

TAKE THE CHALLENGE

When you go camping, what do you take to light your way in the darkness?

CHECK IT OUT

The Lord had a very special way to lead His children in their wilderness journey. Draw a line from each of the pictures below to the time God used this to lead them.

LEd them
by day

LEd them
by night

MAKE YOUR CHOICE

What does God use to lead me in my spiritual walk today?
(Hint: See Psalm 119:105.)

_____

_____

SATURDAY   Exodus 14:1-14

TAKE THE CHALLENGE

What are you most afraid of?
What really gives you the creeps?

CHECK IT OUT

After the Israelites left _____, _____ decided he did not want the Israelites (his former slaves!) to be gone. He got all of his soldiers together and _____ them. Were the Israelites afraid of the Egyptians? **Yes / No** In verse 14, what did Moses tell them? "_____

_____."

MAKE YOUR CHOICE

What do I need to do when I am afraid? _____

_____ Do I usually do this, or do I worry and think the worst? _____

TODAY'S WILDERNESS MENU
(Sorry, no substitutions)

MANNA – Created fresh daily from Heaven's finest ingredients! Our manna cakes have the same great flaky, pastry-like texture and home-sweetened taste that you've loved for nearly 40 years!

QUAIL – By special request. Spit-roasted to perfection over mesquite coals. Golden brown and crispy outside. Tender and juicy inside. All you can eat.

NEW!

Sunday — Exodus 14:15-31

TAKE THE CHALLENGE

Are you a good swimmer, or are you afraid of deep water?

CHECK IT OUT

Here God provided a way for His children to get away from the pursuing Egyptian army. He demonstrated once again that He was more powerful than they were. What did His protective angel in verse 19 do? _____ _____ What did God use to save His people? _____
What happened to the Egyptians? _____
Did the Israelites trust God after this experience (v. 31)?

MAKE YOUR CHOICE

What has really helped me trust God more in my life?

_____

_____

Exodus 15:1-13

TAKE THE CHALLENGE

What's one of your favorite praise and worship songs?

CHECK IT OUT

Here we see Moses and the Israelites singing a song of praise to God. Pick out one verse of it you really like and write it under the musical lines below.

MAKE YOUR CHOICE

How does this praise verse especially bless my heart and why?

_____

_____

Tuesday Exodus 15:22-27

TAKE THE CHALLENGE

Has your Mom or Dad ever let you be the navigator in the car while you were traveling to a place? Did you help them read the map and figure out which roads to take?

CHECK IT OUT

We see Moses leading Israel from the _____ Sea to the wilderness (desert) of _____. How long did they travel without water? _____ What was wrong with the water in Marah? _____ What did the people do? _____ What did Moses do? _____ Then the Lord told the Israelites to listen to His _____ and do what is _____ in His sight and He would keep them healthy along the way.

MAKE YOUR CHOICE

God introduces them to a new name for Himself here in verse 26. In Hebrew, He calls Himself Jehovah-Raapha. This means "for I am the LORD that _____ thee." When I feel sick or go through a bad health problem, I can turn to the Lord in prayer. He wants to _____ me. 183

wednesday Exodus 16:1-13

TAKE THE CHALLENGE

Is it easier to complain about something or to have a grateful attitude no matter what?

CHECK IT OUT

After the Israelites left Elim, they entered the wilderness (desert) of _____. They had been traveling for about 45 days now. What did the people start complaining about and wishing for (v. 3)? _____
_____ Match the following — God's answer to their grumbling:

_____ In the morning

_____ You will know

_____ At twilight ("even"ing)

A. That I am the LORD your God

B. You will eat meat (flesh)

C. You will be filled with bread

MAKE YOUR CHOICE

Write down five daily blessings you can thank God for right now!
_____ _____ _____ _____
_____ Now, actually thank HIM! And every time you find yourself complaining about something today, stop and thank him for one of these things you wrote down.

Thursday Exodus 16:14-22

TAKE THE CHALLENGE

Why do you think it's good to have your Quiet Time – "eating" out of God's Word – each morning of every day?

CHECK IT OUT

The Lord provided a type of b_____ while they were in the w_____ and the people were to take only enough for _____ day. "Manna" means "what is it?" (v. 15). It tasted like a wafer sweetened with honey. What happened when a person took more than they needed? _____
Did everyone obey? _____

MAKE YOUR CHOICE

Does God expect me to obey all the time or just some-times? _____ Ask God to help you obey Him and your parents today.

FRIDAY — Exodus 16:23-36

TAKE THE CHALLENGE

The Sabbath was the Jewish day of rest and worship. It went from sunset on Friday until sunset on Saturday.

CHECK IT OUT

On only one day a week could the people gather enough for _____ days so they could _____ on the _____ day. There would be no food on the _____ for them to find. What did God ask Moses and Aaron to do with the manna in verse 33? _____

Did they obey? **Yes / No**

MAKE YOUR CHOICE

As Christians, we no longer observe the Sabbath but we worship and res on Sunday, the first day of the week, for that is when _____ arose from the _____. How often do I attend church on Sunday? _____

SATURDAY — Exodus 17:1-16

TAKE THE CHALLENGE

Did you ever sing the little praise song, "Jesus is the Rock of my salvation – His banner over me is love"? You'll see where this song came from in today's passage.

CHECK IT OUT

Find the words that are from this passage in the Word Search below. The words to look for:

water murmured grumbled Egypt
elders Horeb rock Massah Meribah
Rephidim Joshua hands altar stone

```
L G E D E R U M R U M
M R L S G O B E R O H
A U D D Y C O L E E A
S M E N P K F D T R B
S B R A T S T O N E I
A L S H K L W A T E R
H E J O S H U A D W E
A D E R E P H I D I M
B E A L T A R O M K F
```

MAKE YOUR CHOICE

God reveals Himself by another name here, after helping them win the battle against the Amalekites: "Jehovah-Nissi." This name means The LORD is my Banner! Is the Lord MY victory when I go through battles and difficult situations? Yes / No

Exodus 19:1-32:6

ch rt y r c rs

What would you do if you knew that you were going to meet God today? What would you wear? How would you act? In this week's Bible reading, that is exactly what the Israelites had to prepare for!

Sunday   Exodus 19:1-13

TAKE THE CHALLENGE

Wash your clothes, take a bath, and brush your hair!

CHECK IT OUT

Your parents occasionally tell you to take a shower, wash your hair, and put on clean clothes. God was the one telling the Israelites to do this in today's reading. Why did they have to get all cleaned up? (See v. 11.) _____

What did the people have to be careful not to do (v. 12)? _____

Why?_____

MAKE YOUR CHOICE

Write down two specific commands that God has given me to obey in His Word?

_____

Ask your parent to pray with you that you will have an obedient spirit.

monday

Exodus 19:14-25

TAKE THE CHALLENGE

Thunder, lightning, thick clouds, an earthquake, thick smoke, and a trumpet blast!

CHECK IT OUT

What would you do if you were at the base of this mountain as all the things above were happening? Would you want to: (circle one) run - hide - scream - hug your mom or pray? What would happen to the people if they tried to reach God by climbing the mountain (v. 24)? _____

MAKE YOUR CHOICE

What are some praise songs that I can think of that describe God's power? Here are a couple of examples: "My God is so Big, so Strong and so Mighty, there's nothing my God cannot do!" "Our God is an Awesome God, He Reigns from Heaven above, with wisdom, power and love, our God is an Awesome God!" My favorite power praise song is _____. Take time right now to sing a praise song to God and thank Him for His mighty power!

Tuesday   Exodus 20:1-17

TAKE THE CHALLENGE

The perfect 10!

CHECK IT OUT

The Ten Commandments are listed in today's passage. Match the command to the order in which it was given.

Don't misuse God's name.	1
Honor your father and mother.	2
Don't murder.	3
Have no gods before Me.	4
Don't lie.	5
Don't steal.	6
Don't worship idols.	7
Don't covet.	8
Keep the Sabbath day holy.	9
Don't commit adultery.	10

MAKE YOUR CHOICE

Why is it important for me to obey God every day? _____

Write Exodus 19:5 here to remind me what God promises as a result of obedience.

" _____

wednesday — Exodus 24:3-12

What can wash away my sin? Nothing but the blood of Jesus!

CHECK IT OUT

In today's reading, Moses conducts a strange ritual with the Israelites. What is the first thing he does in verse 4?

_____

What does he have young Israelite men do in verse 5?

_____

What strange thing did he do with half of the animal blood?_____ What did he do with the other half?_____

MAKE YOUR CHOICE

Wow...wouldn't it be strange (and kind of gross) to be sprinkled with animal blood? However, this strange ritual symbolized that an animal had died to cover the Israelites' sins. When Jesus came to earth, He became the ultimate sacrifice for my sin. If I have asked Jesus to forgive my sin and be my Savior, then He has become the acceptable sacrifice to God for my sin. He literally took my place on the cross. How does this make me feel?_____

Thursday — Exodus 24:15-25:9

TAKE THE CHALLENGE

What can I bring to God?

CHECK IT OUT

How long was Moses on the mountain with God? _____

What things did God instruct Moses that the people could bring for an offering to Him? _____

_____ What were the offerings to be for?

_____

MAKE YOUR CHOICE

What can I give God? If I have a paper route, birthday money, babysitting money, or odd job money, I should give a portion of that money to God. How much should I give? Ask your parents, Olympian leader, or Sunday school teacher for advice. This week I want to give $_____ in the offering or to a missionary.

FRIDAY — Exodus 25:10-22

A special chest for special things!

God gives Moses the instructions for building the Ark of the Covenant. This would be the chest that would hold some very special things - like the actual stone tablets with the Ten Commandments written on them. What kind of wood should the ark be made of? _____ What would the rings, poles, and cover of the ark be made with? _____ Who would actually meet with Moses and speak to him between the cherubim on top of the ark? _____

As special as this ark was, God says that if I know Jesus as my Savior, I am His treasured possession. Has someone said something lately that has made me feel bad? _____ No matter what others say about me, God says He loves me and that I am LESPAIC:
___ ___ ___ ___ ___ ___ ___ ___

SATURDAY — Exodus 31:12-32:6

TAKE THE CHALLENGE — I didn't do it! It wasn't me!

Moses has been given the Ten Commandments on stone tablets by God. What were the people doing while Moses was gone? _____ Who made the golden calf? _____ Whom did Aaron say that the golden calf was? _____ Do you think that he really believed that? _____ Look back to Exodus 24:9-10. What did Aaron see on that day? _____ How could he forget that so quickly? _____

As humans, we are quick to forget the goodness and majesty of God. What is something that has happened to me lately that reminded me of God's goodness? _____
_____ I prayed and God did this amazing thing for me:
_____

Have you ever been camping? Did you help set up the tent? The tabernacle was like a big, ornate tent so that the Israelites could easily move it when they moved from place to place. This week we see Moses hard at work. There are many lessons for us from this as well!

Sunday Exodus 32:7-20

TAKE THE CHALLENGE ## Golden Calf = Big Trouble

CHECK IT OUT

God was so angry at the Israelites for their sin that He was ready to destroy them. Moses prayed for the people and God relented. What did Moses do to the stone tablets when he saw the people's sin?

_____

What did he do to the golden calf?_____
_____ What did he make the people do with the powder?_____

MAKE YOUR CHOICE

Was Moses anger justified? _____ Do I get angry easily?_____ Does my anger please God? _____
How does it make the person I am angry at feel? _____
I will ask God to help me to control my temper right now.

monday

Exodus 33:12-23

TAKE THE CHALLENGE Please go with us!

CHECK IT OUT

Moses wanted the presence of the Lord to go with them as they headed to the Promised Land. He also asked a special request of the Lord verse 18. He asked God to "s _ _ _ m _ your / thy g _ _ _ ." What did God say that He would allow Moses to see? _____ Why couldn't he see more of God? _____

MAKE YOUR CHOICE If I know Jesus as my Savior, He is always with me! What promise does Hebrews 13:5b make about Jesus? "_____
_____ "

Tuesday Exodus 34:1-17

TAKE THE CHALLENGE Come back up the mountain!

CHECK IT OUT

God now gives Moses some instructions for the journey. Fill in the blanks with God's instructions for Moses.
Verse 12 - Don't make a _____ with foreigners. Verse 13 - Destroy their _____.
Verse 14 - Don't worship _____ _____.
Verse 15 - Don't make a _____ with any foreign nation. Verse 17- Don't make any _____.
These are just some of God's instructions to Moses.

MAKE YOUR CHOICE What are some of God's instructions for me that He gives in His Word? Check out Ephesians 6:1 and write it here: "_____
_____ "

191

wednesday   Exodus 34:18-35

What happened to your face?

CHECK IT OUT

There was a definite way that the people could tell
that Moses had been with God... he glowed!
What did Moses wear over his face? _____
Why did he wear it?_____
When did he take it off?_____

MAKE YOUR CHOICE

Is there a definite way that people can tell when I have spent time with
Jesus?_____ Do I think, act, and speak differently?_____
Do I notice a difference in my behavior when I don't spend time with God?
_____

Thursday   Exodus 40:1-16

This is a "set up"!

CHECK IT OUT

Moses is given directions by God to set up the tabernacle.
Crack the code below to find out what Moses did:

___ ___ ___ ___ ___   ___ ___ ___   ___ ___ ___ ___ ___   ___ ___ ___   ___ ___ ___
9 11 13 4 13   3 6 3   7 15 13 14   1 13   14 5 4

___ ___ ___ ___   ___ ___ ___ ___ ___ ___ ___ ___   ___ ___ ___
8 11 12 3   2 11 9 9 1 10 3 4 3   5 6 9

A=1 C=2 D=3 E=4 H=5 I=6 J=7 L=8 M=9
N=10 O=11 R=12 S=13 T=14 U=15

MAKE YOUR CHOICE

Do I always do just as I should? _____ What is one area where I often
DON'T do as I should?_____ Does this please
God?_____ Write your prayer to God about this here:
_____

192

FRIDAY   Exodus 40:17-27

Let's set up the church?!?

Moses is setting up the tabernacle just "as the Lord commanded" him. How many times does this phrase appear in this passage? _____ Today, we don't have to be in church to meet with God. The tabernacle in Moses' time was _____ home on earth - where His presence would dwell. _____ took care to follow God's instructions exactly regarding the tabernacle.

When I am asked to do something by a parent, teacher or coach, how do I react? Do I follow instructions exactly as Moses did? Or do I fuss, fume and get put out when I'm asked to do something that I don't like? One chore that I don't like to do is _____. I will ask God to help me to do this job cheerfully next time.

SATURDAY   Exodus 40:28-38

Who needs a GPS?

Today some cars have built in electronic maps that are linked to satellites to help give us directions. The Israelites didn't need that! What filled the tabernacle when Moses finished it (v. 34)? _____ What did it take the shape of? _____ What would happen when it was time for the Israelites to move to a new place? _____

How does God guide me today? (Circle all that apply) the newspaper -- the Bible — godly people — prayer — fortune cookies -- TV commercials

45 WEEKLY PASSAGES COVERED
Philippians 1:1-2:23

c h r t y r c r s

Can you imagine a jailbird writing letters from his prison cell to churches? - And a jailor writing to a church? - Check out Acts 16:23-34 to get the whole story of this very thing happening! Bet you didn't know that the First Christian Church of Philippi started with a jailor and his family who received Christ as Savior right in jail!!

Sunday   Philippians 1:1-7

TAKE THE CHALLENGE

Whom have you written a letter or email message to lately? Do you ever write someone just to encourage them or make them feel better?

CHECK IT OUT

Well, the Apostle Paul is writing this letter to the new group of believers at Philippi — the Philippian church. Can you complete the blanks below to complete the letter?

PRISON OF PHILIPPI

FROM: _____ and _____, _____ of _____ _____ TO: All the _____ in _____ _____ (who/ which are) at_____, including the _____ and _____ BLESSING: _____ and peace to you from God our _____ and from the _____ Jesus _____ THANKS: It_____ God for you and I always p_____ for you. PROMISE: I'm confident that He who began a _____ _____ in you will perform (perfect or complete) it until the _____ of _____ _____.

MAKE YOUR CHOICE

Two names of Christians that I thank God for are: _____ and _____. Two people I pray for regularly are: _____ and _____. I will put these names in the prayer section of my Quiet Time, if they are not already there.

monday

Philippians 1:8-14

TAKE THE CHALLENGE

What kinds of requests do you pray for your Christian friends?

CHECK IT OUT

Paul prayed for these new believers that _____ would _____ more and more so that they'd make wise and pure choices; and that they'd be (v. 11) _____ with the _____ of _____ that comes through Christ — for the _____ and _____ of God.

MAKE YOUR CHOICE

Look at verse 14. Paul says here that being chained in prison had given him and others more opportunities to share the Gospel. With whom have I been afraid to share Christ's love? _____
I will pray now for courage to witness to this person.

Tuesday

Philippians 1:15-21

TAKE THE CHALLENGE

Have you ever thought about what it would be like to die? Who or what do you live for? What would you die for?

CHECK IT OUT

Look at verse 20. Paul's main purpose in life was to see Christ _____ in and through his body. But he was ready either way! Decode Paul's purpose statement or main mission below.

"# ▫ $ ♥ ▫ ☺ △ ♥ ▫ ! ♫ > △ ♫ □

▼ ∞ $ ♫ □ ♥ + ↔ ☼ ♥ ▫ ☼ ♫ △ ♫ □

▲ + ♫ ↔ ."

+	▼	☼	△	#	▲	∞	♫	!	☺	↔	▫	$	□	♥	>
A	C	D	E	F	G	H	I	L	M	N	O	R	S	T	V

MAKE YOUR CHOICE

How do I know that I'm ready to go to Heaven if I should die?
_____

Right now, how is my life glorifying or magnifying Christ?
_____

wednesday — Philippians 1:22-30

TAKE THE CHALLENGE

Do you have a difficult time making decisions sometimes? Think of something you already had to make a choice about today.

CHECK IT OUT

Fill in the blanks from the following word list: live, die, Christ, flesh, joy, faith, gospel. Paul was having a hard time deciding whether he wanted to _____ or _____. He knew that to die meant he would depart from this world and be with _____ (v. 23). But he knew he needed to remain or abide in his _____ (v. 24) so he could continue to help these new believers in their progress and _____ of faith. He wanted them to be united together in their battle ("contending"/"striving") for the _____ of the _____ (v. 27b).

MAKE YOUR CHOICE

Write out the words of verse 29, putting "me" in place of "you": "_____ _____." Am I willing to suffer or die for my Savior? Yes / No / Maybe

Thursday — Philippians 2:1-8

TAKE THE CHALLENGE

Rate yourself on the following scale by putting an X on the line where you think you are:

_____

SELFISH   SELF-CENTERED   HUMBLE   SELFLESS

CHECK IT OUT

Rate each of the following either an SA (for selfish attitude) or CA (for Christ-like attitude):

_____ Tender/compassionate   _____ Argumentative
_____ Others first   _____ Loving
_____ Conceited   _____ Serving others
_____ Ambitious   _____ Proud
_____ Obedient   _____ Vain
_____ Humble   _____ Unkind

MAKE YOUR CHOICE

In these verses I see what a perfect example Christ set for me in the area of selfless humility. Instead of WWJD ("What Would Jesus Do?"), maybe I first need to tell myself WWJT ("What Would Jesus **Think**?"). What can I do everyday to help me think more like Jesus? _____

FRIDAY — Philippians 2:9-16

TAKE THE CHALLENGE
What have you already found yourself complaining or fussing about today?

CHECK IT OUT
As I yield to God, He works in me to do His _____ in and through my life. If I am in His will, I'll do all things (everything) without _____ or _____. God wants His children to be blameless and _____ in the middle of a _____ and _____ nation/generation - this dark old world — in which we live. We can shine as His lights or stars as we are "holding _____ the word of _____ " (v. 16)!

MAKE YOUR CHOICE
When others, especially those who are without Christ, watch and listen to me, do they see and hear a negative, complaining person or a happy, positive Christian who shares God's Word? _____
Why? _____

SATURDAY — Philippians 2:17-23

TAKE THE CHALLENGE
Do you have any friends who truly stand up for Christ and live for Him?

CHECK IT OUT
What good friend did Paul want to send to help the Philippian believers in his own absence (while in prison)? _____ Put an X through the things that do not describe this young man.

Would share good, happy news about them / Liked to sing / Wrote poetry / Did what Jesus wanted instead of what he wanted / Cared for others, like Paul did / Worked as a tentmaker / Like a son to Paul / A very old man / Served in the work of the Gospel / Had proved himself

MAKE YOUR CHOICE
What are at least three good qualities I need to look for in a good friend?
1) _____
2) _____
3) _____

c h r t y r c r s

What do you know about Paul, the author of this letter?

- ✓ He was an apostle of Jesus.
- ✓ He had died and come back to life.
- ✓ He had actually seen and heard Jesus from Heaven.
- ✓ He was in a Roman prison when he wrote this letter.
- ✓ He had some type of physical handicap.
- ✓ He was actually the first foreign missionary to the Gentiles all over the western world of his day!

Sunday — Philippians 2:24-30

TAKE THE CHALLENGE

How would you like to have a first name like Epaphroditus? Maybe he was called Epap for short! Check him out in today's verses!

CHECK IT OUT

In the word puzzle below, circle all the descriptive words that applied to Paul's trusted friend and co-worker, Epaphroditus. (There are at least seven)

```
A B F E L L O W S O L D I E R
S L D E F G H I J K B L L M E
O W V U T S W R Q P R O L N G
R X Y L A B O R E R O Z A B N
R E P A P H R O D I T U S C I
O F G H Z Y K U R Q H N M D S
W S I C K X E T S P E O L E S
E D C B A W R V C A R E D F E
C H R I S T I A N K J I H G M
```

MAKE YOUR CHOICE

What can I do today to help or encourage one of the leaders in my church, my pastor, or one of my Bible Club coaches?

Philippians 3:1-6

TAKE THE CHALLENGE

What are you really good at doing? Do you ever get proud of your accomplishments in that area?

CHECK IT OUT

Even though the very intelligent and gifted Apostle Paul could make a long list of his worldly accomplishments before he knew Christ as Savior (see verses 4-6), he boiled everything down to three important truths here that we as believers need to remember: (1) Verse 1- "Finally, my _____, _____ in the _____!"
(2) Verse 3c – "_____ in _____ _____."
(3) Verse 3d – "Put (or have) no _____ in the _____."

MAKE YOUR CHOICE

Instead of bragging about what I can do, I need to rejoice and glory in what _____ is doing in my life! Write down one thing I can brag about Jesus today: _____

Tuesday   Philippians 3:7-14

TAKE THE CHALLENGE

What are some things you'd do well to forget – and some things you really need to remember or focus on?

CHECK IT OUT

Paul sort of divides the truly important things in life from that which we'd do just as well to put behind us. Next to the phrases below, put one of the following three letters beside them. Put a V (for very important), an I (for important) or a U (unimportant).

_____ Sharing in Christ's sufferings and death.

_____ All I've accomplished or attained (apprehended)

_____ The earthly things that are to my profit or gain

_____ Knowing Jesus Christ as my Lord

_____ Being resurrected from the dead

_____ Everything this world has to offer

_____ Pressing on to earn or take hold of all God has for me

_____ The things of the past, which are behind me

_____ Straining or reaching for what's ahead – His prize for me

MAKE YOUR CHOICE

Write out the first half of verse 8: "_____
_____Lord."

Can I truly say this about myself? _____ Why or why not? _____

199

wednesday — Philippians 3:15-21

TAKE THE CHALLENGE — If you asked someone else to watch your life and do what you do, what would they be like?

CHECK IT OUT — What did Paul tell the Philippian believers to do in verse 17? (Circle one.) To be like Christ / To follow His example / To be steadfast. Then Paul describes those who are "enemies of the cross of Christ." (Match them below.)

Their glory	On earthly things.
Their end or destiny	Is in their shame.
Their god	Is their belly/stomach/appetite.
Their mind	Is destruction.

MAKE YOUR CHOICE — What kind of example am I setting for those who watch my life?_____

Who might be following my example?_____

Thursday — Philippians 4:1-7

TAKE THE CHALLENGE — Do you ever get anxious or nervous about something that might happen or about a school test?

CHECK IT OUT — Paul gives us the remedy for anxiety in verses 4-7. First he tells us to "_____in the _____ always." Then he reminds us in verse 5 that the LORD is _____. In verse 6 we are instructed to take our worries, anxieties, or cares to God, "in every thing by _____ and _____ with _____", as we share our requests with Him. What will "keep" or "guard" our hearts as we pray? "The _____ of _____."

MAKE YOUR CHOICE — Something I often worry about is: _____ _____ Today, instead of worrying or being anxious, I choose to _____, _____ and give _____ to God.

FRIDAY
Philippians 4:8-13

TAKE THE CHALLENGE

What do you do when your thoughts take a turn for the worse – when they get more and more sad and negative?

CHECK IT OUT

Follow the nine steps up the ladder to godly thoughts (v. 8). Write each of the qualities we're told to think about on the rungs of the ladder.

Whatever is...

MAKE YOUR CHOICE

Write out the wonderful words of verse 13 here:

"_____

_____ "

Do I really believe this verse I just wrote out? Yes / No

SATURDAY
Philippians 4:14-23

TAKE THE CHALLENGE

When was the last time you gave a love offering to God to help a missionary or church project?

CHECK IT OUT

In verses 14 to 18, Paul is instructing these believers about why and how to give to God's work. We can never out-give God. What is the wonderful promise made in verse 19 to believers who are not selfish but giving?

"_____ my _____ _____ _____ all your _____ according to His [glorious] riches in glory in Jesus Christ!"

MAKE YOUR CHOICE

I will pray about what God would have me give to Him. How much money would I like to save to give to His work? _____

201

47 WEEKLY PASSAGES COVERED
Ecclesiastes 1:1 – 12:14

christ your course

Ecclesiastes is a Greek word meaning *The Preacher.* It suggests someone who addresses or teaches a group of people. This book is quite different in tone from all the other *Wisdom Literature* books in the Bible. The *author,* according to chapter 1:1, is *David's son* or *King Solomon.* This book is the *testimony* of the wisest man in the world – but one who found out that life on this earth is completely empty without God in the center!

Sunday   Ecclesiastes 1:1-18

TAKE THE CHALLENGE

Everything on earth seems to go round and round, and yet never comes to a conclusion, says the wise King. You clean your room, and then you have to clean it again two days later. Mom washes the clothes and they're all dirty again before she knows it. The same clothing styles that were in 10 years ago are back!

CHECK IT OUT

As we go through this book together, reading all the things with which Solomon tried to fill his life, we will see how disappointed and distrustful he became. The phrase used most in the book is the theme. It is in verse 2:

"_____," says the Preacher (Teacher), _____."

As you continue through Ecclesiastes, circle in your Bible every time you see this phrase. Let's see how many times it occurs!

MAKE YOUR CHOICE

Verse 11 speaks of those who pass away and how quickly they are forgotten. What loved one of mine has died?_____
Do I still remember him and talk about him? Yes / No
Why? _____

monday — Ecclesiastes 2:1-11

TAKE THE CHALLENGE

"Party Hearty!" Have you ever heard kids talk about their partying? Do partying and doing only fun things bring real joy to your heart?

CHECK IT OUT

Solomon shares in these verses about his pursuit of mirth or pleasure Circle the things he used to try to fill his life in the area of PLEASURE: Laughter Wine (alcohol)   Folly   New cars   Movies   Houses   Beautiful gardens & vineyards   Owning slaves or servants   Pools of water   Animals Trampolines   Silver & gold (lots of money)   Men & women singers

But when you get to verse 11, what was his sad conclusion? All [everything] was _____.

MAKE YOUR CHOICE

What do some of my friends or neighbors do to try to make themselves happy? _____ Does it satisfy them or do they have to go find something else to buy or do after that?

Tuesday — Ecclesiastes 2:12-26

TAKE THE CHALLENGE

"Is That All There Is?" is the name of a song from several years back. It describes the emptiness of life after you've tried everything you know to give you happiness and peace.

CHECK IT OUT

Solomon tried to decide which of these three was better (circle what he decided on): madness / folly / wisdom . But then in verses 15-16, he says that _____, also, is _____.

What are the sad words he ends with in verse 17: "_____." Who does he conclude is the only One Who can give true wisdom, knowledge, and joy (happiness) in verses 24-25? _____

MAKE YOUR CHOICE

How many times have I seen the word vanity or meaningless so far in this testimony of Solomon? _____ If he was the richest and wisest man who ever lived, AND he knew riches and knowledge didn't satisfy, then where do I need to look for real happiness and joy? _____

203

wednesday — Ecclesiastes 3:1-14

TAKE THE CHALLENGE

"To Everything – turn, turn, turn – There is a Season – turn, turn, turn – And a time for every purpose under Heaven." This was a very popular song in the 60's, sung by a famous band of that era.

CHECK IT OUT

In today's passage, Solomon pauses to share a poem. How many times does he use the phrase "a time" in this poem? _____ Match the following by connecting them with lines.

A TIME:		A TIME:	
To be born		To heal	
To mourn		To laugh	
To weep		For peace	
To kill		To die	
To love		To dance	
For war		To hate	

MAKE YOUR CHOICE

Check out verses 13-14! Solomon says that everything good is really a _____ of _____ and that everything God does will be _____. God does it so that men – I – will _____. How do I show God I fear – honor or revere – Him for Who He is?

Thursday — Ecclesiastes 5:1-7

TAKE THE CHALLENGE

Have you ever made a pact or secret promise to a friend? Did you keep it?

CHECK IT OUT

In this passage, Solomon talks about how we are to behave and what our attitude should be when we go to worship in the _____ of _____ (our church): (1) v.1 - Go to _____ not to show God how much we have to give. (2) v. 2 - Don't _____ too much! (3) v.3 - Don't make a commitment or vow to God that you don't plan to _____.

MAKE YOUR CHOICE

Did you ever go forward and commit your life to Christ — maybe at church or at a campfire service? Yes / No   How are you doing at KEEPING that vow or commitment to God? _____
What do I need to change? _____

FRIDAY
Ecclesiastes 11:7-10

"Life is short – and then you die." This is a quote seen on many teens' tee shirts. It shows what they believe about the uselessness – or briefness of this life on earth.

CHECK IT OUT

Solomon is reminding us in verses 7 – 8 that life is sweet sometimes and dark at other times. But one thing we know for sure: Compared with eternity, life is very _____ and will end for everyone! He reminds young people that we can enjoy all of life's pleasures down here, but if we live for pleasure and meaningless things, "God will _____ _____ _____ _____" (v. 9).

MAKE YOUR CHOICE

Could I face my Maker today with a clear conscience that I have lived for Him and not myself? Yes/ No What needs to change in my thinking and the way I'm living these days?

_____

SATURDAY
Ecclesiastes 12:1-14

TAKE THE CHALLENGE

When's the last time you observed an elderly person? What did you learn about aging from watching them?

CHECK IT OUT

The two most important verses in Solomon's testimony are in this chapter – at the beginning and at the end. The first is: "_____ _____ _____ in the _____ of _____ _____." Then he describes what old age looks like so that you are motivated to live for and serve God NOW while you have a good mind and good health. Match the problem of old age with the descriptive picture Solomon paints here:

____ Grinders cease because they are few
____ Windows are darkened
____ All their bird songs grow faint
____ The almond tree blossoms
____ The grasshopper drags himself along

A - Can't hear well anymore
B - Body bent and walks slowly
C - Arm & hands grow weak
D - Teeth become fewer
E - Hair turns white
F - Eyesight fails

MAKE YOUR CHOICE

What does King Solomon – the richest and wisest man who ever lived – end his book with? "Let us _____ the _____ of the _____ _____: _____ God, and _____ His _____: for this is the whole duty of man." Fearing God means I'm always aware of His presence in my life, and I try to do everything I do and say for His glory. Do I really fear God? Yes/ No What elderly person can I reach out to with God's love this week?

_____

christycrrs

We now begin to study a book written by the Apostle Paul. Paul was a servant of Jesus and an apostle. "Apostle" means "one who is sent." Paul was sent to preach the Gospel. "Gospel" means "good news".. Paul was sent to preach the Good News of Jesus to the Romans.

Sunday   Romans 1:1-7

TAKE THE CHALLENGE

Do you like to get letters in the mail?

CHECK IT OUT

In this passage, Paul begins his letter to the Romans. What do we learn about Paul in verse 1? _____
_____

What three things do we learn about Jesus in verses 3 and 4? _____
_____

MAKE YOUR CHOICE

Paul felt called to serve Jesus and to share the Gospel with others. Do I know Jesus as my Savior? _____ If I do, who could I share the Gospel with this week? _____

monday
Romans 1:8-17

TAKE THE CHALLENGE

Can you imagine being on the news all over the world?

CHECK IT OUT

The Christians in Rome were famous! Their faith was being reported or told about all over the _____ _____! This was encouraging for Paul to hear these great reports of their faith and spiritual growth! In verse 9, what did Paul say he constantly did for the Roman Christians? _____

_____

MAKE YOUR CHOICE

Who are three people I pray for regularly?
1) _____
2) _____
3) _____

Tuesday
Romans 1:18-32

TAKE THE CHALLENGE

What can we know about God through creation?

CHECK IT OUT

According to verse 20, two things that everyone knows about God when they look around at the world are His eternal p _ _ _ _ and divine nature or Godhead. Knowing this, also from verse 20, we are all " w_____ e_____!"

MAKE YOUR CHOICE

What's one thing in nature that really reminds me of God's mighty power? _____

wednesday — Romans 2:1-13

TAKE THE CHALLENGE

Who is the only one who is qualified to judge our lives?

CHECK IT OUT

Do you judge others? Do you compare yourself with them and say, "at least I'm not as bad as they are!" Yes / No
The Bible says that the only One who is qualified to judge man's sin is God. All sinners need to "repent" or turn around and start on a new path. According to verse 4, God's _____ leads people to _____.
What do you know about God from verse 11? _____
_____

MAKE YOUR CHOICE

I should not judge and criticize others because _____ is the true Judge. He is the only fair judge. To whom have I been unfair or critical of lately? _____

Thursday — Romans 2:17-24

TAKE THE CHALLENGE

What does it mean to be a hypocrite?

CHECK IT OUT

A hypocrite is someone who says one thing and then does something else. In this passage the _____ were talking about how religious they were, but their actions were very different from the way they talked. Put an X over the things they condemned or preached against, yet did themselves:

loving others   **faithfulness**   **stealing**

idol worship   **serving God**   **breaking God's law**

MAKE YOUR CHOICE

What do I tell others not to do, that I do myself? _____
_____

Could I be a hypocrite sometimes? Yes / No / Maybe

FRIDAY — Romans 3:5-8

TAKE THE CHALLENGE

Should we sin so that others can see how wonderful God is to forgive us?

CHECK IT OUT

The answer to the above question is "of course not"! _____ still has consequences, even though God has promised to _____ us (1 John 1:9). How can God be totally loving and totally just all at the same time? The only way that God could be both at once is to condemn us as sinners, and then take the punishment on Himself. He is the only sinless One. Who is the only One God can use to be totally loving and totally just? (Circle one)   **Paul   Angels   Jesus Christ**

MAKE YOUR CHOICE

Circle below some ways that I can grow in my love for Jesus:
Say nasty things---Read my Bible---Watch bad TV---Pray---Tell my friends about Jesus---Have a bad attitude--- Respect my teachers---Lie to my parents---Be kind to others---Be quick to get angry

SATURDAY — Romans 3:9-20

TAKE THE CHALLENGE

Can we be good enough to get into Heaven?

CHECK IT OUT

Write out Romans 3:10: _____
_____

How many people are righteous? _____

How many people seek God (v.11)? _____

How many people do good (v. 12)? _____

MAKE YOUR CHOICE

The only way to go to Heaven someday when your life on this earth is over is to know Jesus as your personal Savior from sin. Write out Jesus' own words in John 14:6 here: "_____"
Am I sure that I will go to Heaven when my life here on earth is over? If not, why not ask Jesus to forgive my sin and be my Savior today?

ch rt y r c rs

There are two terms used in this week's passage that were used in other places in Bible times as well.

The word "justified" is borrowed from the law court. The judge declares that the person on trial has no legal charges against him.

The word "redemption" is borrowed from the slave market. It means "to buy someone out of slavery."

Sunday   Romans 3:21-31

TAKE THE CHALLENGE

Imagine that you are a slave and that you have just been set free!

CHECK IT OUT

Verse 24 talks about two words that are important in understanding salvation. What are they?

R _ _ _ _ _ _ _ _ _ and J _ _ _ _ _ _ _ The meanings of the words are found in Chart Your Course above.

MAKE YOUR CHOICE

If redemption means, to buy someone out of slavery, from what types of slavery has Jesus delivered me? _____

_____

Romans 4:1-12

TAKE THE CHALLENGE

What makes you happy?

CHECK IT OUT

The word blessed also means happy. Write verse 7 here: "_____

_____

_____ "

MAKE YOUR CHOICE

According to this verse what do I have to be happy about?

_____

_____

Tuesday Romans 4:13-25

TAKE THE CHALLENGE

Who is the most powerful superhero you can think of?

CHECK IT OUT

How powerful is God? He is more powerful than any superhero or strong man. Even though He is the most powerful Being in the universe, He still wants to be your friend. And because God is so powerful, He Is able to keep all His _____ (v. 21) to us. What two Old Testament people did God keep His promise to in these verses? _____ and _____ Nothing will ever stop God. He will always keep His promises to us...He never fails!

MAKE YOUR CHOICE

Write out verse 21 here:" _____

_____ "

What promise has God kept to me? _____

wednesday — Romans 5:1-11

TAKE THE CHALLENGE
Can you be joyful even when bad things happen to you?

CHECK IT OUT

Here Paul says that since we've been j_____ by or through f_____, we have _____ with _____ through our _____ _____ _____ _____. Then he shares two things we can rejoice in: (1) In the h_____ of the g_____ of G_____ (v. 2b) (2) Our _____ (v. 3a). Follow the trail in verses 3b – 5a: and fill in the blanks.

Tribulation or sufferings ⟶ p_____

_____ ⟶ h_____ ⟶ _____

_____ ⟶ l_____

MAKE YOUR CHOICE

Verse 8 tells us that God showed His love for us in that while we were still _____, He sent Jesus to _____ for us. Jesus loved us even though we weren't loveable. Praise Him now for loving you and sending Jesus to die for you!

Thursday — Romans 5:12-21

TAKE THE CHALLENGE
How many times have you heard the story of Adam and Eve?

CHECK IT OUT

This passage compares _____ to Jesus. How are Adam and Jesus alike? Put an A before those that refer to Adam and a J for those that refer to Jesus.
Through this person . . .

_____ sin entered the world

_____ salvation was available to all

_____ all people were made sinners

_____ all people could now choose salvation

MAKE YOUR CHOICE

How does Jesus' gift and Adam's sin affect my life?

_____

_____

FRIDAY
Romans 6:1-12

TAKE THE CHALLENGE

What do you struggle with?

CHECK IT OUT

If you know Jesus as your Savior, you should live like it! Read verse 11 again. What should we consider ourselves dead to? _____ What should we consider ourselves alive to? _____

We should live in obedience to God and His Word and not continue to keep on living in _____.

What do I find hard to overcome? Is there one sin that seems to trouble me? Write that sin here: _____ Now, ask God to help you overcome that sin with His help. Remember, ". . . Greater is He that is in you, than he that is in the world." (1 John 4:4)

SATURDAY
Romans 6:13-23

TAKE THE CHALLENGE

What is a wage?

CHECK IT OUT

A wage is payment for work that you have done. According to verse 23, the payment for our sin is _____. But the news doesn't end there! Write what the last part of verse 23 says "but _____

_____

_____"

What is the "gift of God"? _____

Who can I share God's wonderful gift of salvation with this week? _____

50

ch rt y r c rs

Life
Peace
Death
Fun
Sin
Purity

Our world today can be confusing at times. We want to live for God, but so often, the things of the world sidetrack us. Keep your eyes open this week to the difference life "in the Spirit" can make!

Sunday · Romans 7:7-13

TAKE THE CHALLENGE

Do you Know the Ten Commandments?

CHECK IT OUT

The Ten Commandments are the (circle one) suggestions / rules / letters that God gave to Moses on tablets of (circle one) paper / cement / stone. The Pharisees and religious leaders used to think that if they obeyed _____ _____ all the time that they could go to Heaven. Obeying the Law of God is good — but it will not keep us from (circle one) sinning / rejoicing / falling. It is actually more like a mirror for our hearts to show us our _____ and that no one can keep _____ _____ perfectly. What does this bring about or produce according to verse 13? (circle one) joy / salvation / death.

MAKE YOUR CHOICE

Could I ever obey God's Laws enough to go to Heaven? _____ Who do I need to thank for keeping the Law perfectly, and then dying in my place? _____

Romans 7:14-25

TAKE THE CHALLENGE Do you like riddles?

CHECK IT OUT

In this passage, it is almost like Paul is talking in riddles! He wants to do _____, but he can't seem to do it. He doesn't want to do _____, but he does it anyway. In verse 25, whom does Paul thank for rescuing him? _____

MAKE YOUR CHOICE

Have I ever felt like Paul in these verses? _____ Write below some things I don't want to do, but I often do them anyway: _____ _____ Now pray and ask God to help you not do the things you shouldn't, and help you do the things you should!

Tuesday Romans 8:5-11

TAKE THE CHALLENGE What do you like to think about?

CHECK IT OUT

What does verse 6 say about the mind of the sinful man? _____

What does verse 6 say about the mind controlled by the Spirit? _____

If you know Jesus as your Savior, then you have the Holy Spirit living inside you to help you know right and wrong, and to give you the strength to say no to sin and yes to obeying God.

MAKE YOUR CHOICE

It is important that I confess my sin to God when I do something that displeases Him or goes against His Word. Is there anything I need to confess to God today? _____

215

What do you look forward to?

Perhaps you look forward to a special trip or an upcoming holiday. Sometimes our life on this earth is hard. People get sick and die, our friends say mean things about us, or we fight with our brothers and sisters. When hard things happen to us, in a way, we are suffering. What does verse 18 say about suffering? _____

When Paul talks about the "glory that shall be revealed in us," he is talking about one day, when what Jesus has done for us will be fully known, and we can spend eternity in Heaven with Him.

MAKE YOUR CHOICE

Am I suffering in some way? Am I going through hard things that sometimes seem too much for me? Write about them here: _____
_____ I must remember that Jesus is always with me, to help me, guide me, and strengthen me for the day ahead. I will take time right now to talk to Jesus about my sufferings...because He cares for me!

Thursday   Romans 8:26-39

What do you pray about?

Sometimes we have a hard time knowing what to pray about. The Bible says that even when we don't know what or how to pray, the _____ helps us pray to God in words that we cannot even say. Look at verse 27. Who knows the mind of the Spirit? _____
_____ Who intercedes (prays) for the saints (Christians) according to God's will? _____

MAKE YOUR CHOICE

Am I having a hard time knowing what to pray about or how to say it? Yes / No Remember that God, the Holy Spirit, is there to help me pray. Prayer is simply one friend talking to another friend. If I know Jesus as my Savior, He is my _____. I can talk to Him in prayer at any time, in any place, for any reason. He _____ me, and loves to talk to me!

FRIDAY Romans 9:1-16

TAKE THE CHALLENGE

Is there anyone you love very much who does not know Jesus as Savior yet?

CHECK IT OUT

Do you have relatives or family members who don't know Jesus as their Savior?

Check It Out: Paul was Jewish by birth. Many of the _____ did not believe that _____ was the promised Messiah. Paul was very sad about this and wanted his fellow Jews to be _____ so badly that he said in verse 3 that he would be willing to what? _____

MAKE YOUR CHOICE

Even though Paul wished to take his friends' place, he couldn't. Do I have a friend or family member whom I'd like to be saved? Write his/her name here: _____
Write his/her name in your prayer pages right now.

SATURDAY Romans 9:17-33

TAKE THE CHALLENGE

Can God use bad people to show His glory?

CHECK IT OUT

_____ was an evil king of Egypt in the Old Testament. He mistreated the _____ and made them his slaves. But even though Pharaoh was powerful, God was _____ powerful. According to verse 17, why does God "raise up" Pharaoh? _____

MAKE YOUR CHOICE

God eventually used Moses to free His people, Israel, from slavery. He showed that He was more powerful than even a powerful king like Pharaoh. Since God is the most powerful in the entire universe, I can trust Him for anything I need. What do I need to trust God with today? _____

WEEKLY PASSAGES COVERED
Romans 10:1-12:21

DO YOU EVER WONDER WHAT GOD'S WILL IS FOR YOUR LIFE?

Try circling the three things below that might be the biggest help to you in finding out God's will !

KNOW Christ as Savior
HeLP Out at Church   Read God's Word
Give Money   Pray and Ask
Be nice to people
Seek Wise Advice from Godly Leaders

Sunday   Romans 10:1-13

TAKE THE CHALLENGE   What kind of person can be saved?

CHECK IT OUT

Do you have to be rich, poor, white, black, short, tall, young, or old to be saved? There is a verse in this passage that answers our question. Write verse 13 here: "_____

_____

_____ "

According to this verse, who can be saved? _____

_____

MAKE YOUR CHOICE

What does it mean to be "saved"? _____

_____ If I were going to explain to my friend how to be saved, what would I say? _____

monday

Romans 10:14-21

Can you hear about something without someone telling you about it?

CHECK IT OUT

How can people be saved if they have never heard about Jesus? _____

How can people hear about Jesus? _____

_____ What do we call people who spend their lives telling others about God and His love for them? _____

MAKE YOUR CHOICE

Name some people I know who spend their life telling other people about Jesus. (It could be my pastor, or a missionary I know.) _____

_____ Take the time to pray for those people right now. Pray that they would present the Gospel clearly to others.

Tuesday

Romans 11:1-12

TAKE THE CHALLENGE What does grace mean?

CHECK IT OUT

Some people define grace as

_____ took the punishment for all of our sins on the cross. We then have to accept His free gift of salvation by believing in Jesus to save us from our sin. This is grace. We all deserve to be punished for our _____. But God put our punishment on _____, Who had never _____. Jesus took this punishment for us. This is _ _ _ _ _.

God's
Riches
At
Christ's
Expense

MAKE YOUR CHOICE

What does God's grace mean to me? _____

_____ How do I feel knowing that Jesus took the punishment that I deserve?

_____ How does it make me want to

live knowing all this? _____ 219

wednesday

Romans 11:13-24

TAKE THE CHALLENGE

Can you be kind and severe (stern), all at the same time?

CHECK IT OUT

Verse 22 says to consider or behold "the goodness (kindness) and severity (sternness) of God." What do you think this means? _____ _____ Maybe you can think of your parents when you think about this phrase. Your parents are probably kind to you. They love you and provide for your needs and even sometimes your wants. They give you gifts and presents on holidays, and they make your meals and wash your clothes. In a word, they take care of you. But they can also be stern if they need to be, scolding you if you disobey, don't do your homework, make your bed, or eat the right foods. Why? Because your parents _____ you, and they know you need kindness in your life, but sometimes you need _____, too, to keep you safe, healthy, and to help you grow into the person God wants you to be.

MAKE YOUR CHOICE

How has God shown that He is good and kind in my life? _____
_____
_____

Thursday

Romans 11:25-36

TAKE THE CHALLENGE

How does God show that He is a stern God who wants to help me grow in Him?

CHECK IT OUT

Verses 33-36 are so beautiful! They read like a verse of poetry! Pick out something Paul says about God in these verses and write it here: _____
_____
_____
_____

MAKE YOUR CHOICE

I will take time during my prayer time to praise God for the things I have written above. My God is Awesome!...Why not take time to tell Him so right now?

FRIDAY — Romans 12:1-8

TAKE THE CHALLENGE

Do you like Jell-O®?

CHECK IT OUT

The phrase "conformed to this world" (or the pattern of this world) literally means don't let the world squeeze you into its mold. Like Jell-O® takes on the form of the mold you pour it into, we also can start looking like the world and not like children of God. If we are truly God's children, then we will act like it. Others will be able to see a difference in the way we act, speak, and react in every situation. Write out what God longs for us to do in verse 1:

"_____

_____"

MAKE YOUR CHOICE

Put an X on the line that shows how much of you (energy, money, thoughts) you have given or surrendered to God.

Not surrendered at all   Fully surrendered

| 10% | 30% | 50% | 70% | 90% |

So are you "conformed to this world" or "a living sacrifice"? _____

SATURDAY — Romans 12:9-21

TAKE THE CHALLENGE

How can you heap "burning coals" on your enemy's head?

CHECK IT OUT

What is God saying in verse 20? Is He really saying that you should go out and dump hot coals on your enemy's head? The answer, of course, is no. But when you treat your enemies, or those who treat you badly, with kindness, it makes them feel bad about their actions as well...just like burning coals. Go back through this passage and write down every phrase that has to do with how we should treat others...whether they're enemies or friends. Here's one example to start you off: Verse 10b: Be devoted to one another with brotherly love. Verse 16:_____

Verses 14 and 17:_____

Verses 18 and 19:_____

MAKE YOUR CHOICE

So how am I doing? Is there someone in my school or neighborhood that I don't get along with? _____ What can I do about this? _____

chrty rcrs

Here the Apostle Paul is, coming to the end of a long and very important letter he was writing to believers in the great city of Rome, Italy. They had banded together to form local churches and were meeting in secret because of the severe persecution from the power-driven emperor and Roman government. . . And yet Paul will even address the issue of the need to respect and obey government officials!

Sunday   Romans 13:1-7

TAKE THE CHALLENGE   Who is the leader of your country?

CHECK IT OUT

God has set up leaders in places of authority, not only in your country, but also in your life. Who are the authorities in your life? Who is/are your:

Teacher _____

Parents _____

Principal _____

Pastor _____

MAKE YOUR CHOICE

We all have people in our lives that God has set in authority over us. It is our job as God's children to respect these authorities and obey them. Put their names in your prayer pages and pray for them each week!

monday

Romans 14:1-12

TAKE THE CHALLENGE

What do you think your best friend should do differently or better in his/her life?

CHECK IT OUT

How about it? Are we responsible to tell our friends what to do and how to act? _____ No, unless what they're doing is sin, and goes against God's Word. Write verse 12 here: "_____

_____

_____

_____

_____ "

MAKE YOUR CHOICE

Who will I have to answer for when I stand before God's throne someday? _____ Knowing that, what do I need to change? _____

Tuesday

Romans 14:13-23

TAKE THE CHALLENGE

Are you a peaceful person?

CHECK IT OUT

Write verse 19 here:" _____

_____ " _____

_____ " What does it mean to "make every effort", "follow after" or "pursue" here? _____

_____ Is there a situation in your life at school or home that isn't very peaceful?

_____

MAKE YOUR CHOICE

What efforts am I making to be peaceful? _____
Am I thinking about others, or just about myself and how this affects me? _____ Am I quick to be angry? _____ Do I pick fights with others at school or in my family? _____
How will I change?

wednesday   Romans 15:1-16

TAKE THE CHALLENGE   Why was the Bible written?

CHECK IT OUT

Find the answer to the Take the Challenge question in verse 4 and write your answer here: _____

_____

_____

How can we learn from the people that are written about in the Bible? _____

How can their lives encourage us today?

The Bible is so important in helping me live a godly Christian life today. It offers me hope when I am discouraged. It tells me of God's love when I feel like no one loves me. What does the Bible mean to me? _____
_____ I must thank God today during my prayer time for giving me His Word, the Bible.

Thursday   Romans 15:17-33

TAKE THE CHALLENGE   Do you like to travel?

CHECK IT OUT

Paul went to many different places to tell people about Jesus. Some of the places we recognize today, but others sound odd to us. Look back through this passage again, and circle at least four places in the word puzzle that Paul traveled to.

```
M D E L A E H T A L O
I A X A M P L E E D S
M Z C D F T L M N Y P
U S E E V A N T E D A
C I S L D A I B R Q I
I C U C U O R T V X N
R K S F P S N N H O R
Y L A E I P T I G E I
L U R A C H A I A V O
L E L A D N A T I O N
I J M E L A S U R E J
```

Do I like to go to different places? _____ Does going to a foreign land sound exciting to me? _____ Have I ever thought about being a missionary when I grow up? _____ Have I prayed about this and asked God if He would like me to be a missionary one day for Him? If He says yes, am I willing to go and tell others about Him, wherever He asks me to go? _____

FRIDAY — Romans 16:1-16

What are the names of your best friends?

CHECK IT OUT

Paul is finishing his letter to the Romans and is now sending greetings along to his friends. Wow! His friends sure had some different names compared to what we are used to! Some of his friends meant a lot to him for different reasons. List some of the reasons Paul thought a lot of the following people: Priscilla and Aquila (v. 3) _____

Andronicus and Junia (v. 7) _____

Tryphena and Tryphosa (v. 12) _____

MAKE YOUR CHOICE

What do my friends do for me that make them such good friends? _____
_____ What do I do for my friends that makes me a good friend to them? _____
_____

SATURDAY — Romans 16:17-27

TAKE THE CHALLENGE

Do you know anyone whom you think is truly wise?

CHECK IT OUT

Who is the only One who is truly wise (v. 27)? _____
_____ Who is the only One who can truly help me when I have a problem or trial? _____ What is He called in verse 20? "The _____ of _____." Who will He one day destroy? _____

MAKE YOUR CHOICE

What problem or burden do I need to take to Him in prayer? _____
_____

225

WORD OF LIFE Weekly
Quiet Time Passages

To allow you to see which books of the Bible you will be covering in this year's Quiet Time please refer to the weekly passages listed below. These are the same passages used in all Word of Life Quiet Times. And if you would like to listen to the daily Quiet Time radio broadcasts the corresponding dates are listed as well.

Week 1	Aug 26 – Sep 1	Psalms 26:1-31:24
Week 2	Sep 2 – Sep 8	Psalms 32:1-35:28
Week 3	Sep 9 – Sep 15	Psalms 36:1-39:13
Week 4	Sep 16 – Sep 22	Psalms 40:1-45:17
Week 5	Sep 23 – Sep 29	Psalms 46:1-50:23
Week 6	Sep 30 – Oct 6	2 Corinthians 1:1-4:18
Week 7	Oct 7 – Oct 13	2 Corinthians 5:1-8:24
Week 8	Oct 14 – Oct 20	2 Corinthians 9:1-13:14
Week 9	Oct 21 – Oct 27	Genesis 1:1-5:32
Week 10	Oct 28 – Nov 3	Genesis 6:1-11:9
Week 11	Nov 4 – Nov 10	Genesis 12:1-22:18
Week 12	Nov 11 – Nov 17	Genesis 24:1-27:33
Week 13	Nov 18 – Nov 24	Genesis 27;34-35:15
Week 14	Nov 25 – Dec 1	Genesis 37:1-41:36
Week 15	Dec 2 – Dec 8	Genesis 41:37-44:34
Week 16	Dec 9 – Dec 15	Genesis 45:1-50:26
Week 17	Dec 16 – Dec 22	Matthew 1:1-4:25
Week 18	Dec 23 – Dec 29	Matthew 5:1-7:29
Week 19	Dec 30 – Jan 5	Matthew 8:1-10:31
Week 20	Jan 6 – Jan 12	Matthew 10:32-12:50
Week 21	Jan 13 – Jan 19	Matthew 13:1-15:39
Week 22	Jan 20 – Jan 26	Matthew 16:1-19:15
Week 23	Jan 27 – Feb 2	Matthew 19:16-22:33
Week 24	Feb 3 – Feb 9	Matthew 22:34-24:51
Week 25	Feb 10 – Feb 16	Matthew 25:1-26:56
Week 26	Feb 17 – Feb 23	Matthew 26:57-28:20
Week 27	Feb 24 – Mar 1	James 1:1-3:10
Week 28	Mar 2 – Mar 8	James 3:11-5:20
Week 29	Mar 9 – Mar 15	Proverbs 6:1-8:11
Week 30	Mar 16 – Mar 22	Proverbs 8:12-10:32
Week 31	Mar 23 – Mar 29	1 Chronicles 10:13-17:27
Week 32	Mar 30 – Apr 5	1 Chronicles 21:18-29:30
Week 33	Apr 6 – Apr 12	2 Chronicles 1:1-7:11
Week 34	Apr 13 – Apr 19	2 Chronicles 7:12-20:30
Week 35	Apr 20 – Apr 26	2 Chronicles 29:1-36:21
Week 36	Apr 27 – May 3	1 Peter 1:1-3:7
Week 37	May 4 – May 10	1 Peter 3:8-5:14
Week 38	May 11 – May 17	Exodus 1:1-4:17
Week 39	May 18 – May 24	Exodus 4:18-8:15
Week 40	May 25 – May 31	Exodus 8:16-11:10
Week 41	Jun 1 – Jun 7	Exodus 12:1-14:14
Week 42	Jun 8 – Jun 14	Exodus 14:15-17:16
Week 43	Jun 15 – Jun 21	Exodus 19:1-32:6
Week 44	Jun 22 – Jun 28	Exodus 32:7-40:38
Week 45	Jun 29 – Jul 5	Philippians 1:1-2:23
Week 46	Jul 6 – Jul 12	Philippians 2:24-4:23
Week 47	Jul 13 – Jul 19	Ecclesiastes 1:1-12:14
Week 48	Jul 20 – Jul 26	Romans 1:1-3:20
Week 49	Jul 27 – Aug 2	Romans 3:21-6:23
Week 50	Aug 3 – Aug 9	Romans 7:1-9:33
Week 51	Aug 10 – Aug 16	Romans 10:1-12:21
Week 52	Aug 17 – Aug 23	Romans 13:1-16:27